also by Joseph Granda-Padron
available from Lulu Press

Abstraction (2005)

Veneer (2005)

Omega (2007)

Forgotten (2007)

CHOICE

Poems

By

Joseph Granda-Padron

Copyright © 2007 by Joseph Carlos Padron

ISBN: 978-0-6151-5715-3

All rights reserved. No parts of this book may be reproduced in any form or by any electronic or mechanical means, including information storage and retrieval systems, without permission in writing from the publisher, except by a reviewer, who may quote brief passages in a review. Any members of educational institutions wishing to photocopy part or all of the work for class room use, or publishers, who would like to obtain permission to include the work in an anthology, should send their inquiries via email to: carlosgp1430@yahoo.com.

This collection is dedicated to

William & Myrna

My parents,

I followed my dreams

And I became a poet.

Thank you both

For teaching me

How to read

&

Write.

Table Of Contents

A Small Forward   i
Acknowledgements   iii

When Sleep Comes Upon Me   1
With Teachers   2
I Don't Want To Fall   3
More Rain   5
You're Growing   7
Fake   9
What If…   11
Lighted Stars   12
A Song   13
I Have Seen   15
I Found   17
The Rush   18
Ordinary Originality   19
White Boys   21
Ouija Board   23
Alcoholics   25
Spent Time   30

The Park   31
Desire to Vanish   33
I'm At A Loss For Words   34
Loud Voices   36
So Broken   37
The Category   38
The Film   39
The Coming   40
Strangest   42
A Few Days   44
God Answered   46
Regret   47
Mad Woman   50
Tell Me   52
Blessing   53
Fade Off   54
The Pain In My Head And I Cry   56
The Sky   58
Letter For Isis: Part One   59
Letter For Isis: Part Two   62
Letter For Isis: Part Three   65
Assistance   67
Angry Cousin   70
Sushi   71
I Haven't Had A Drink In 5 Days   72
The Babies Are Crying   74
Faggot   75
The Molded Man   78
Imagined Reality   79
My Body Is Toxic   81
Wasted Potential?   82

Cigarettes & Drink &   83
Gutter of Wonder   84
Infected With Poetry   85
Twisted And The Song Is In My Head   87
O But I Have Not Shown You   89
Such Horror   91
She Had   93
My Cousin   95
Devil In My Bedroom   97
You Have Not Lost Me   99
Two Raccoons   101
The Long Wait   102
Useless   103
Dry Trip   104
A Real Hero   105
Dry   109
God Speaks   111
To The Anti-Bukowski Publishers   112
Together   113
Watermelon   115
Fio   117
Nailed   120
April 1, 2007   122
A Poem To My Past   125
I Have Inspired   126
Sooner or Later   129
They're So Many   130
Fine Quality Paper   131
Well-Up   133
O How The World Has Left Me   134

Endangered Species   136
Arthur   138
I Am Chaos   140
The Ass Is Out   141
Sometimes Late At Night   142
You Push Them Aside   143
Voyage   146
The Cats   147
They Tell Me   149
I've Started   150
Consideration   151
Jungle   153
Sloth   155
Regression   156
Tremendous   157
Why Even...   159
Nicky   162
For Your Self   165
Bullshit   167
Playing At God   170
Getting Married   172
My Sister   174
Reading At Night   175
Prepared   178
Pinky   180
Upset   181
Goose Flesh   183
Age And I'm Fast Approaching   185
Text Messaged   187
Yes... I Want To   189

Curse Me, My Beauty   191
Explicit   193
Vonnegut Dead At 84   194
Fall Again   196
Every Step Forward   197
Bane Of Existence   198
I Walk Myself Into Pain   200
Princess   201
Smile   203
Poet   204
Working In A Cafeteria Full Of Children   205
The Reason   206
Lost Souls   209
Needed Time Together   210
Granda-Padron, The Simpleton   212
Routine Of The Scheme   215
A Choice   217
Given All   218
Marriage   220
Depression   221
Father Guardian   222
At The Funeral & Nonina   223
Don't Worry   225
Pablo Neruda   226
Toni, My Poetess   228
Enough Ammo   230
Kindness   233
Isis & Her Bicycle   234
Shit Smeared   235
Sense   237

Back At It Again   238
Not Enough   240
A Break In The Routine   242
The Barbarian At The Theater   244
A Trip Into Jersey   245
Machine Throat   247
Simplistic Nature   249
Man vs. Child   250
A Family Veneer   252
All You Can Try   253
Give Your Ass To Everything   255
Old Chick With Style   256
A Taste & Then: Return   257
One Month Clean   259
Fist Fight & Death Stayed Home   260
Can't Write What You Don't Know   261
Self-Destructive   262
Music: Just Right   264
Tattooed   265
Persecutor   267
I May Be Drunk   269
Because Whatever The Fuck   271
Vero & The Discovery   273
Pitiful Men   275
My Little Brother   276
Branded   277
The Sand In-between My Toes   278
Faces   280
"Fuck it!"   281
Alex Has Everything Under Control   283

Heroes **284**
Problem + Bullets = Intelligence **287**
School, Again **289**
Manic Depressive **290**
Tai Chi Bullshit **292**
Ghost With Drink & Smoke **294**
Illiterate Retard **296**
Started On The Seroquel **298**
Song Of Sparrows **300**
Toni **302**
Immaculate Drink **304**
Lust Is Such A Fucked-Up Sin **306**
Don't Confuse Sympathy **309**
15 Minutes **310**
Birth Of A Murderer **312**
Aunt Margie, I Miss You **313**
A Call Of Unity **315**
A Toast Of Pride **317**
Preparation For School **318**
Too Poor For School **320**
The Violence Of Gods **321**
The Poet Needs Pain **322**
Mismatched Slippers **324**
Ejaculate On The Bee's **326**
Boxing Gloves **327**
The Alcoholic Of Awe **328**
Madness Of The Masses **329**
Drugged Voyeur **331**
Kylie **332**
A Burning Tree **334**

As A Nothing **336**
Mother Murderer **338**
The Silence **340**
My Last Fling **342**

You remember…

When I'm gone…

You remember how much

I loved you.

—Margaret Padron (1960-2005)

A Small Forward

In 2005 I suffered the loss of my grandmother & my aunt. Up until this tragedy in my life I had put writing behind me. I procrastinated. I drank & smoked as much as I could. Though I had the love of my family, I found it so very hard to cope with this period in my life.

It was during this turmoil that I decided to finish my novel 'ABSTRACTION' and begin writing poetry. I succeeded and now, two years later, though I still grieve for my lost loved ones, though I drink beer like a fish, smoke like a chimney, I have never once felt that they weren't somehow looking over me.

So, now, I use the year 2005 as a sort of birthday. It is the year my poet-self was born. It is the year I truly felt my childhood die. And the year I decided I wasn't going to try writing but actually write.

This book is a product of then, a continuation if you will, of a promise I made to myself. I'll never give-up. I will never stop fighting.

In the words of Che: "Hasta la victoria siempre!"

Acknowledgements

This is my fifth book and the one I never expected to see. It's been a long journey for me and there are always those that deserve thanks.

Isis, my daughter, everyday you're in my life I find strength. Vero, my wife, forgive me the madness I always seem to cause. Rafael Sr. and Ivonne Granda for always being there for me.

Aunt Vicky, Uncle Alex, Luis, Little Alex, I love you all. Each of you carried me when I tried to destroy myself and for that I am overtaken with appreciation.

—Joseph Granda-Padron
July 2007

CHOICE

When Sleep Comes Upon Me

When sleep comes upon me
It's in terrible sweats.
Wake every night
As if suffering,
Dreamless suffering,
Was / is my eternal burden.

Vero doesn't know
Because I haven't told her.
It's not that I'm embarrassed.
No, never embarrassed. Many of
The eldest living
Still haven't a clue
As how to approach
This unspoken obligation
Of sleep.

To hell with it!
Of every practice I've
Ever practiced in life
Sleep is the most
Unwanted desire I have,
Unwanted so viciously,
So dearly,
I drink the lager
To forget this urge
To embrace
The sweat of suffering.

With Teachers

On the bus
With teachers
Who haven't cars
And I think of Vero
And how hard it was for her.

But looking now
There's a difference
Between these people and my love.
She tries to be friendly and put
Aside the pigheadedness that
Takes over the soul
With bachelor degrees
And shit like that.
Awards
Merits
Honors
Fuck if I know!
I'm simply poet
In love with a woman
Responsible for teaching
Tomorrow's burden
Or successes.

I can't wait to get
Off this bus.

I Don't Want To Fall

I don't want to fall into this
Torturous routine like
Everyday everything.

I need change and stars.
Man, the stars you see
When the forty ounce is finished
And all that remains
All that deserves freedom
Is the greatness
Left after the drink.

Alcoholistic dreams
On carpets of hydro.
The smell alone a gift
Of gods and love and
Rage and 'fuck-you' if
You want to take my
Self – myself and what
Makes me different.

I want nothing with
The path of the many,
The hell of everyday
Everything, every piece
Of lost desire wanting
To hold me down,
Keep me down.

I don't want to fall,
Ever,
Into this torturous routine.

Fucked up broken
Routine!

More Rain

It hasn't rained like this
In over a year and a half.
Everything / everyone
Swollen with water
Swollen with the H2o.

Umbrellas are doing very little
And people (not myself)
Have even decided not to fight
The torrential downpour
Drowning the city today.

Today… I wonder if
When I was born
It rained like today?
Almost thirty years now.

Fought with the Board of Education
Since 2000.
Been married to my love
Since 2001.
Been a father to my daughter
Since 2003.
Lost Nonina and Aunt Margie
In 2005.
And I've written four books
Four books…

Life is like rain –
Rain drops –
Each drop an event
And no drop alike.
I've begun my fifth
Book (my fourth collection
Of poetry).

I hope for more rain.

You're Growing
for Isis Margaret Padron

And how each day I wake
You take from me a little more
Then I have to give…
And how I'd give you everything
In me so willingly.

I watch you sitting at your table
Playing with your toys
Watching the television
Rubbing your feet on the floor
Hair a tangled mess.

I wish William and Myrna
My parents; your grandparents
Could have known you
Or felt for just a second
How it feels to love you.

When I watch you run
Or we play 'Tag' and you call
Me the monster, fleeing,
Running as fast as you can
And the sparkle of joy in your eye…

Every time we play
That silly old game
I find it harder and harder

To hold back my tears
And yes, sometimes I have to

Turn away from you
Because I haven't the strength
To hold the tears back.
I get embarrassed and I wipe
Them away before you see them.

It's great being a father
Watching you grow
Hearing you talk
Seeing the world through
Your eyes.

When we go to the park
This afternoon
I will thank God for your happiness.
I will thank him for your life.
And I will likely turn away
To wipe away
My embarrassment.

Fake

Fake muthafucka
Lookin' at me
Sayin' hello and handin'
Me his hand.

How does a man turn
His back on a friend
For money?
How is that honorable?

Then the asshole
Extends his hand to you
And you're supposed to take it like
Hell, like nothin' in the whole
World is wrong.

Fake smile
And Asshole asks
How my daughter is doing.
I want to spit his face
But I need my job

So I shake his hand
And tell him fine.
Then he asks "How you doing, Carlos?"
And I say:
"Workin' on a poem about
Fake people."

He smiles and we part ways and
In my head, as I watch him disappear
I scream aloud:
'You fake muthafucka!'

But then who's the fake?
Him for betraying friendship
Or me for not confronting
The betrayal?
Fuck it!

Fuck him!

What If...

Joey said to me once
"If our family were around
in the Middle Ages
they would have killed every
one of us."

"Why?" I ask.

"Look how strong we are
when we're together.
We would have been the
True birth of Mafioso."

"I think you might be right." I say.

"Sure as shit I'm right.
You'd be dead.
I'd be dead.
All of us."

"What about now?"

"Now, if there were a catastrophe
where millions died
just one of us would take over
the world."

I shook my head and said: "You're right."

Lighted Stars

But when you stand there
Inhaling the smoke of your cigarette
On your porch,
Or your balcony,
Or simply at your window,
In the sky just as in our heart
The lighted stars of our hope

The hatred of our song
Standing in mid air, not moving,
Untouched by the sameness
Of society, untouched by our
Own past and its wretched ways

I look towards them
Beer in hand
Cigarette in hand,
This is what so many before me
Saw. They held the same dreams I hold
The same song I now sing.
Loved and hated
Preserved and killed.
I will walk the realms
Of intoxication
And believe, with spark in my eyes,
That my dreams are real
And up there somewhere with the stars
I could one day know them.

A Song

Tiesto,
Oakenfold,
Taucher,
And the Thrillseekers.
All in my ears and
Guiding me into the next phase
Of life. That next song
With hypnotizing beats
And meaning and rhythm.

I haven't met many fans
Of Trance music.
Such a sad result
For such a beautiful and intriguing
Form of music.

I listen to Trance
All day and night and when the world
Seems to me to be on another
Channel.
"Did I dream?"
"Southern Sun?"
"Winter Love?"
What ever the flow or cause
It radiates so deep within me.
The notes on beats and tunes
On bliss and proper form and perfect
Realization of movement

Gift of now and yesterday
Meaning as much as tomorrow.

I work to the melodies of great DJ's
And flow
Flow
With immeasurable amounts of talent.
I will let the Trance carry me through
The storm of lager and
Procrastination.

Move me.

I Have Seen

I have seen the crash of tomorrow
On streams of blood.

My hands move over the keyboard
As if born to the keys
And merged together
With the substance on anger and
Fate and lost desire.

I have seen the crash of tomorrow
On reams of page and gift of song.

My soul moves me into sadness
And depression and I just don't want to
Understand how all of this
Came about
Ever came to be
Ever should have been.

The days
Move into the world a little faster
And end a little slower.
I move with the poem and the lager
Fills me with proper conception
And never ending notions of
'What if?'

I have seen the crash of tomorrow
On streams of blood.

I will write it all down
On pages of pulp and madness
And there will be no looking back
No regret of tomorrow and
What ever the hell
I was to have made of it.

I Found

Vero told me
Writers are crazy
And they haven't sense enough
To be normal.

As a writer of my own
Elected caliber
I can honestly say
We have to be 'crazy'
Because it's society's term
Of 'crazy' that defines us.

We write the truth
As we and only we can see it.
We explore and experience
What so many others
Would shy away from.

So, yes, I haven't the sense
To be what she calls normal.
Probably and hopefully never will
Have normal attached to anything
That I am.

Fucketyfuckphuckfuckyphuck!

The Rush

He owed the Russian mobsters
A few measly hundred dollars
And he didn't want to die.

They looked at him, saw in him a job
They had to have done
And handed him a blade.

"We will give you three names." They said.
"And this blade." Handing him the blade.
"And when you finish… your debt
will be paid."

So it was
He knifed three men
He didn't know,
Never saw in his life,
And cleared his name.

Ordinary Originality

I saw a film today
That said there is no longer
Any originality left in our world.

There have always been others
Who have reluctantly
Walked the path we each
With all respects
Walk now.

This is truth!
All truth speaking is simple
Honesty.
Truth.
These are core elements
Of banality.

My alcoholism is nothing new.
Millions before me
And after me shall embrace
The toxic elixir, smile
O how they'll smile,
And yes, banality…
Sad originality.

What proves the film wrong is this:
If I were banal then this poem wouldn't be.
If you were banal

You wouldn't be reading this poem.
The film that I saw
Was wrong.
This very world we live in
Is originality in itself.

But then again…
To tell you the truth,
If alcoholism is unoriginal
This poem was indeed written
By a boring copycat,
A bootleg poet!

White Boys

Playing basketball
And flexing their muscles
Watching the underage beauties
Staring back at them.
I envy them…

Every single one of them.
They have rich parents and
Good clothing and
Cars… such incredible cars.

How can I not envy
What I don't have and what I want?
Do you know how I envy those
Young men and their women?

I would devour their flesh
With the philosophy that I'd
Gain their strengths with their
Consumption. I'd eat their women.
I'd eat their parents.
Cut each person into segments
Like cutlets
And dine each night
Like an Egyptian pharaoh.

The cops would question me and
Ask just why it was I ate them

And I'd say because I wanted
Rich parents
Good clothing
Incredible cars.

I'd say I was starving for a taste
Of what it means to live the high
Life in life.

Playing basketball
Flexing their muscles
I'd have taken a hammer
To each of their faces
If it hadn't been for me being
Half white.

Before I left his apartment
William once told me I'd come
To hate who I was.
He was right.

Ouija Board

As children
My sister & I believed
In anything we read.
Reality was discouraging.

My sister bought a book of witchcraft
And I managed to get my hands
On a Ouija board. We were so excited
The day we decided to combine the two.

We had so many dreams
At that tender and fragile age.
She wanted to be rich
And I…
I wanted to live forever.

Board in front of us
Book well studied
We had a plan to sell our
Souls to the devil
In order to fulfill our dreams.

The ritual was fast
A lit candle in a dark room
With mirrors and fear and hope
We left behind God and
Whatever it was he stood for.

Today, as I look at the roads
We have both traveled
My sister has unbelievable luck
When it comes to gambling and
The attaining of funds.
Money falls from the sky for her.

In my own case,
I have written four books,
This being my fifth,
And know in the years to come
Many will know my name.

I will miss my soul
If it isn't already gone.

Alcoholics

I hate alcoholics so damned much.
Always twitching
When they're sober
Always yearning for a drink
And blaming everything wrong in their
Lives
On any and every thing
Besides
Themselves and their bottle.

They come
To work hung over
Stumbling
On their own steps
And wishing the night before hadn't
Been what it was and waiting for night fall
To try
Again.

They reek
Of addiction and disease
Look like shambles and broken promises
Eyes bloodshot and purple bagged
Always searching for that next
Dream
Inside a bottle that vomits
Lies of freedom
But mocks you

With its elusiveness
& stark refusal to produce positive
Results from any one lie.

Drink after drink
And hope
Washed away in burps and farts
And snores and fist fights and
Sex
And cars and DWI's and
Dance halls and park benches
It'll never be the same and
What you ran from
Will always be there
Trying to pull you back and
Pushing
You further into
The bottle.

I hate them
And how they constantly want
A drink,
They hide a flask on
Their person and always have enough
Change for a refill.
Or ask someone
Some random asshole on the street
For change
"Need to get some food…" the
Alcoholic states.

And the asshole,
Whoever he is,
Will clean his pockets looking to help
This sad excuse for life.

They leave their families and
Have no jobs.
They think they know everything
And they have no hair.
Some even reach a type of
Mixed reality in which they believe
Themselves invincible.

The world will claim them
To be the victims and type
All men of art with its affliction.

I hate alcoholics
Like the moon hates the sun.
Always there following me
Looking at me through my mirror,
Staring
At me like I'm the problem.

The other day
At the meeting when I stood up
In that room full of alcoholics
I grew hate out my eyes and mouth
Stormed out the damned
Meeting hall

With one thing on my
Mind…
Well, two!

Get far away from the assholes
That thought they knew me
And head over to the first store
With a forty ounce
Of any imported
Lager
And guzzle away those
Damned alcoholics
And their comfort
And their drunken stories
And dead faces
And their useless pride
Stink breath
And horrid eyes
And sweaty handshakes
God, how I hate them!

I guzzle my forty
As hard and fast as I can
Because the bastards are trying to RELATE
To me. Like I need relation
Like I want anything to do with them.
They try to tell you they care
Open up arms for hugs
Long looks of supposed understanding
And bullshit like that.

They try to claim all kinds of sober
Days – days without drink and pride
Oozes
OOZES out of their fuckin' faces
Like crap out my ass.

I guzzle the forty.

I guzzle the forty.

I guzzle…

One of them told me I was in denial
And I told him: "What do you know? Asshole!"
And he walked off into the herd of
Other assholes in the meeting hall.

I know tomorrow I'll be hung over
And my eyes will be blood shot
And my breath will stink
But fuck, when the coming of night fall
I'll get a chance at another forty…

And another…

And another…

Etcetcetcetcetcetc!

Spent Time

We spent time together today,
Vero and I.
How we walked fighting the cold
Hand in hand beside one another
Like veterans of hope
And relationship
And trials.

We talked of what it would be like
To retire at 64 or 65
Buy some real estate and
Work on being together
Learning how to fall
Head over heels in love
With each other, again.

It felt good
Those few moments together
Against the cold and the rituals of time
And life and the world around us
And behind us not meaning
A damned thing.
It felt good to be together.

The Park

The children here...
They know only of slides
And swings
And ladders
And poles
And running with
Laughter across their hearts.

They should make a place
Like this
For adults...
Where it'd be mandatory
To spend at least
One day there
A week.
I'd go several times a week.

(Bury treasure in a sandpit
Bounce on the see-saw
Play on the monkey bars
As I did in my youth.
O, how I loved to
Be happy in my youth,
Remember how it was
To be happy & smile for real,
To be full of dreams
And not know what to do
With them all.)

They should make a place
Like this
For adults.
Replace the gym
For a park
With laughter across the
Hearts
Of every unbound member.
I'd go several times a week.

Desire to Vanish

The working week has just begun
And I'm so tired, already.
Not tired of work… never that.
Tired of the sickening routine of it.

What I'd really like to do
Is vanish into some padded
Room where people have been
Known to begin again.
(Bellevue!
And drug induced invisibility.)

I'm At A loss For Words

And can't find the grasp of them.
Wish for a beer
Wish for a pint of whatever
Dog piss or yeast infected cunt
Whatever…
Whatever…

O how my head hurts
And I think it's because I'm caffeine
Deprived and I want coffee
And sex
Doggy style
Blueberry yogurt lathered into
The flesh of her back
Scented with a hint of ass
Passionate ass
On my forehead

And the flavor ripping through my nasal
Passage, filling my lungs
With bliss-bliss-bliss

But I still want a beer
Or a foot massage
And this is my little word exercise
Get my juices flowing and my cock at
AHH – TENNN – HUTT!

This is no masterpiece
Never claimed my work master material
Never claimed title of master

And I was once known as
The Botanical Garden Flasher
Balls flapping in the air
Naked amongst the poison oak & pine trees.

I have…
I have not…
I don't care if you believe
And don't forget this poem
Began
With a loss for words.

Loud Voices

Damned if I need a break from the chaos
Damned if the chaos needs me.
Always belching up
Terrible strings of word
And word meaning nothing at all.

My brain was once very capable
And strong enough to overcome the madness
And so & so lurking into my ear
Corrupting my brain
Nerves
Spine
Train of thought.

Then the screaming begins
Then it ends and begins again
And again…
And again…
HELP! My sweet song
You hurt me with your
Indistinguishable hymn.

I grow weary of this…
I grow old with impatience & a yearning
For silence.

So Broken

This place we're at
Is as broken
As the currents
Of my wretched heart - soul
And whatever the hell else makes
Me who you think I am.

The walls bleed with Vodka and I want
It more and more and more and
When you look at me
I don't have to confess...
You already know
It's on my breath.

I wanted to sing you a song
Before we made love
But the drink carried me off and
Deserted
Me half alive on a dream
Across the world.

Tomorrow,
Hung over and torn with regret,
I shall look at you
And wish the pain of my
Beaten miserable past
Would abandon its torment of
Our future.

Category

They gave me a look of wonder
Because my skin didn't
Match theirs.
I was a shade too light.
A shade not from their
Category or their liking.
The music wrapped around my soul
And the rhythm
Consumed
My thoughts and body.
Did it matter my skin wasn't theirs?
Did color matter?
Never.
I felt the words of the song
Reggae
And the blood shed and the suffering
Ulterior motives and sweeping clean
The soul.
Upon talking, my mouth moving,
They realized
I was their brother.
Perhaps a shade too light
But nevertheless,
Their brother.

The Film

Last night
I saw a film
About a killer who killed
For no reason at all.
Half way through
I wanted
To leave because:
How I hate
Movies like that.

Needless murder.
Useless.

Yes,
I'd like to get away
From this city
And its sick stage of entertainment.
Go off to a place
Where
People love one another
And acceptance of such a sort
As murder
Would be a fairy tale.

O, I paid $10 for the ticket
So I sat through
The whole
Film.

The Coming

You feel it
Changing you
Molding you into something
Lost
Gone
Passionate.

My poems have become
Questionable.
People read them and then
Refuse to recognize me.
It's as if their
Offended by MY words.

I did not ask them to read the page
I did not ask them to indulge
In words that flowed
From me.
Fuck them!
They read my work and find a truth
They fear in reality

And so fear my words.
I came into their hands
With a fury they themselves didn't
Recognize.
Now, they avoid me
As if I am virus.

Truth is a virus that infects
That must be cut away
That can't see the light of day.

I do not care for their indifferences
Or their refusals of me.
I have indulged myself
Deep into my dreams
And refuse to believe
I should halt
And
Look back into what never
Mattered:
Critique.

Strangest

Strangest thing today.
There was a slight snow
Storm
And throughout it all
The sun blazed
& flourished.
Sweet melody of world's beauty
O how I longed for days like this
While drunk,
Instead,
I find them
Sober and normal.

Perhaps God has given me light
When I feel
Most depressed
And darkness when I feel
Most alive.

That sun sure looked beautiful
Bouncing
Off the snowflakes
And flakes bouncing off me
Walking across
The city pavement
By stores
And people I wanted
My life to never know end

Never. Such sights
To live through them
And bare witness…

My dreams
Mean to me as much
As this blizzard sunshine
As much as Dostoevsky's 'White Night'
Or Hemingway's 'Farewell to Arms'
O how I have got to take
My time
Feel it out… this weather
&
When I get home
I'll tell Isis
Every little detail
Confess to her the love I felt
For the world just then
As the blizzard blew
And the sun fought the elements
From millions & millions
Of miles away
And won…

I'm glad to live here:
A broken city
But,
A beautiful
World.

A Few Days

A few days ago, when Vero found
My gloves and smiled
I thought
It's going to be strange
Wearing gloves
I've forgotten how?
Put them on…
Hold something…
Protection from the cold…

I took them from her
Kissed her
& when she walked away
The pair in my hands
Me staring down at them
I tossed them
To the side.

Today, ten degrees outside
I decided that when I went out to face
The world
It'd be with my new found gloves.
Wearing them
In the treacherous cold
I thought of Vero
And how I'd thank her
For saving my hands

And I guess it's one of those
You don't appreciate
Something
Until you really put it through
Good use.
So
While I was admiring my new gloves
I just happened to walk by
A lady with bare hands
Staring
Intently at mine.

Quickly pocketing my hands
She looked at me
Murder in her gaze
I walked faster
And then thought:
WOW!
Vero turned me into a target
Of murder.
She's forever playing
Silly games of the sort
With me.

God Answered

But what is truly
Remarkable…
What I can't bare to ignore
Is the
FACT
That God has always answered
My prayers.

(Like Vero)

If I am soulless
Then why is it
I feel as if God
Has blessed me?

Why do I grow in love
For Vero & Isis
And continue to despair
For my own will
To survive.

Regret

Today
Looking at Isis
Who was in Vero's arms
I felt like a father.
I told Vero that it's only
When I'm with our daughter
That I feel I don't have to drink.

Our daughter,
Isis
Has taught me of innocence,
Again.
I hold her little body
In my arms and
I love her.

Like her mother
Through all the madness
I've caused
Her love is the only thing
I'm absolutely
Sure
Of.

I've betrayed everyone
In my life
Now & still, but
These two women…

My daughter &
My wife,
They still love me.

They're angels sent to me
By God himself. They
Protect and shelter me
And I truly feel
As if
I give nothing in
Return.
I haunt their steps
With my addictions
My sins.

Vero once told me
After one of our arguments
That she believed, just
As the same with my sister,
I was born
Without
A soul.

I remember performing
A spell during
The early morning of a day
I can barely remember.
My eyes
Stared into a mirror.
I was in a room

Of darkness and my reflection
Was a shadow
In its slick black
False surface.

I stared until the face
In the mirror
Was someone else's…
Then I sold my soul
To be immortal and free
Of my parents.
Reciting some kind of poem
In some strange
African dialect
That night I think
Now
It was the devil I saw
In the mirror

And I'm filled with regret.

Mad Woman

I sit next to a mad woman
Talking to herself in the waiting room
Of Vero's hospital.
We're on a routine visit and:

"You will never live here!" she states.
I can hear her and her thoughts
It's her thoughts I hear.

"The door is locked.
Heavy metal locks…
1…
2…
3…
Across town
If something happens to him
You'll never forgive yourself.
1986!
The coats are inside
The closet." It comes in blurs.

"You take the locks off the door?
Take him to school…
Terminate the lease…
Open the closet…
Hang your coats in the closet
Not on the furniture."

Poor woman.
I feel for her in such a way
I wonder if she's a schizo
She reminds me
Of a slow morning in
December. Cold. Sometimes
Snow & sometimes no snow.

"1…
2…
3…
Over there on 161st."

I've been to 161st
Such a violent place late
At night.

"The door is locked!
Heavy metal locks!
1…
2…
You take the locks off
The door?"

And when the doctor calls her
In to be seen…I thought
I hope he didn't, whoever
He is, take the locks
Off the door.
161st is crazy.

Tell Me

Tell me
Your dreams
My little
Love
And I will
Sacrifice
My life
For them…
For you!

Blessing

I
Do not
Need
The blessings
Of the
Wicked…
For I have
The blessings
Of
God.

Fade Off

I've been told by the lost
That my bloodline is at end.
After my death there shall be
No one to carry my name.

My daughter will take the name
Of some other meaningless
Upon marriage and those
Of our surname
Have forsook the quest
Of child bearing.

There
Are three males
One is gay
One is broken
And the other
Writing this poem
Is an alcoholic grown in age
And confused with
Life.

Where will history place
My blood?
Will it remember the
1st Joseph and his murderous heart?
Or the drug addict seeking
Enlightenment in a crack pipe?

The mad alcoholistic poet?
Or the child looking for freedom
In a plant and pussy?

Will remembrance
Even matter?

I drink iced tea
From a tall glass.
Smoke
Breathe
Hold my beer gut belly
And smile a bit.

My poems
The book in your hand or hands
Is a single piece of
All that's left
Of a family torn
Over decades of punishment.

The Pain In My Head And I Cry

Of saddened days on unquestioned
Existence.

My love, where are my children?
Did I have a son?
Someone to look upon
As my continuation…

I gave to my dreams
A daughter
A maker of life
And my name shall be dead in 30 years
But my blood
Will
Flourish like weed.

And I cherish her for that
I cherish and care so deeply
For her life and smile and
I will look at her until my dieing minute
Like God did the entirety
Of creation
After the seventh day.

There is a throbbing in my forehead
Behind my sinful optics
Tearing into my brain
And down along my spine.

I will not question
I will not falter
Through pain or whatever
I shall remain ever hopeful
Remain ever constant in my quest
To find nothing that hasn't already known
Discovery.

My name shall fall
But my spirit shall infect
With inspiration and hunger
With desire and truth

And when my daughter,
A single child,
Looks out into the world
She will stand the very essence of a man
Built of rebellion and poetry

(The world will tremble at her existence
and regret her not having been born
a man. Her strength… will devour
and I will look down from the heavens
and know all the pain…
the pain in my head…
taught her of life and suffering and
poetry and I will be pleased).

The Sky

In the seduction
Of day
I found the sun
In the promise
Of the night
I found the moon
But of the truth,
There
Is one truth,
They rest in the sky
As one
And not two.

Letter For Isis: Part One

If anything in our lives
Can be said
To be destiny
It's our very
Existence.

What we become
Is our choice
We aren't our parents
You aren't me
And
Likewise
I you.

What is now is this page
And your decision to read
My words.
I love you.

This is my destiny.

In your life
I will
Ask you for nothing
But expect from you
A dependence &
I wouldn't sacrifice for anyone
But you

My child
I wouldn't struggle
With my addictions for anyone
But you.

When you were 2 years of age
I dreamed of you
As a beautiful woman
Drenched in the light of God.

In this dream
I had done what it is
I have always wanted.
I had given into the bottle.
Lying on the pavement of some street
Drunk
I opened my eyes
The two on my face
And the one in my chest
And there you were
Smiling
Helping me to my feet.

I looked upon your face and
Knew you'd come to save me.

This is the image
My savior
My little love
And so this is the man

You have saved.
I am your friend
Your protector
Your father.
I am your love
As well as
Your wrath.
I am your eyes
& your nose
Your strengths & weaknesses
I am your loss and your faith
In the mirror
I am your being
Within your blood
I am the cell.

Letter For Isis: Part Two

(1)
There is great pain in this world
My little love.
People have grown accustomed
To causing sorrow.
(I guess the same could be true
for it's opposite.)
People need pain
In order to feel
Alive
& whether causing it
Or receiving it
Existence of it has to be.

(2)
Romance is a broken creature
The acceptance of it
Is the refusal to accept
Facts.
For the attainment
Of romance a person will abandon
Logic for belief
Truth for falsehood…
Call it blind faith.

Desire can be cut off
As a parasite,
A virus.

"Wanting, hunger, drive,
can all be direct roads
to failure."
Time and strengths of history
Can say this of
Desire = Weakness
(in terms of love).

Friends
Family
Whatever the outside influence
External influences
Demolish the purity
Of love
The most supreme of emotions.

And it is this,
Isis,
These external influences
That will forever and always
Tarnish
Any hope for success
Through love
For it is the strongest
& weakest of mans
Emotions.

So what must one do
In order to overcome this obstacle
Desire

Passion as well
(Being seen
As direct cells of love)?
You mustn't allow
Passionate desire
Or
Desire passion.
Of course
This is easier said then done.
For, like all human beings,
Wanting is inevitable
Almost a sixth sense.

But nonetheless
It can not hold a place in your
Forefront of thought.
You must possess a superior
Splice of life.
You must be what I like to call
A 'Dragon'.

A snake is cunning
And will succeed using any means
Necessary.

A 'Dragon' will use a snake
To achieve its goal and
Should the snake fail
Then:
It is the snake that falls.

Letter For Isis: Part Three

A person that is your friend
Merits all you can give them.
Help unconditionally.
Yes,
Even love
Your friends.
But when a single disappointment
Should occur
Begin to contemplate how
You can use your friendship
With the traitor
To further benefit yourself.
Use them but allow them
To believe you &
Still feel for you the way
They always have
You are 'Dragon' not snake.

This outlook may seem brutal
But it's the only sure solution.
In life you will learn
That *all* people are greedy
And expect from you
Your very soul.

When you encounter people
Refrain from telling them
Anything personal

And if for some reason
This person manages to learn
Of something you don't wish
Known,
Then you must find a way
To render the obtained info
Useless.

(& learn these letters to you
my love.
For love and friendship
Can tear you apart.

I hope as you have done me
In my dream
My letters may save you
In life.)

Assistance

Went out to face the world
Today with a cigarette in
My mouth
And the cold weather flushing
Through my clothes
And into my flesh with no
Regard for my person.

Man stood across the street
Looking at his car
Fists balled up
Looking down at a layer of ice
Keeping his car in park.
He looked around for help
And then back down.

I took another drag on my
Cigarette and noticed in the car
Two children
In the back seat.
They were looking out
Into the cold of the
World
The terrible ice keeping their father
From their journey.

I took a drag
And saw his frustration.

He obviously hadn't a shovel
Because he tried to kick the ice
Away from his tires.
Circling the car
With futile strikes at an element
That cared less.

I took a drag
Thought about a pint & my dreams
And then the children…
They still watched their father
And I took a drag
And started towards him.

"Hey, Brother!" I called.
He looked up and smiled
And I said: "Need a hand?"
"Yes! Thank you so much!"

He leapt into the driver's seat
& I got behind the car
At the trunk and pushed
And pushed
And he gassed it
And they were off and moving
Smoothly over the ice.

The children looked at me
Through the window
And waved goodbye

Took another pull
On my cigarette
And stood on my porch
Looking out at a now
Motionless
Ice covered neighborhood.

I took one last drag & said
While exhaling:
"I hope the kids get to where
they have to go…
all this damned ice."

Angry Cousin

My cousin called me
And with anger in his tone said:
"You made me sound
like a drug addict in your poem!"

I tried to apologize
And he said don't worry about it
But I am left
After that conversation
With a strange sense of confusion.

He talks to me of writing
A book that will shake up society
And wanting to tell the world
To go "fuck itself!"

Then he calls me
With this nonsense
And I have to apologize for
MY WORK!

In my next poem
Consisting of content
Based around him
I will call him a priest
And say he has never taken a shit
In his entire life.

Sushi

Sushi is something else!
O God!
I must have shit blood
For over an hour & a half.

God it was terrible
And I was sure
I'd see that bright light
At the end of some tunnel.

My wife banged on the bathroom
Door
And asked if I was alright
And groaning
And asshole burning
I mumble
I was about to keel over
And bite the dust.

She answered by saying
"Hurry up!"
And suddenly I wasn't
Just shitting blood
But my heart fell out my ass
Too.

I Haven't Had A Drink In 5 Days

Last night 9 people here
In the Bronx
Died in a fire.
8 kids and 1 adult female
Gone with flash and flame and flesh
Curled into nothing but ash.
Fat bubbles on the cooked muscles
Of children and woman.
The city is in mourning
So am I…
I haven't had a drink in 5 days.

My coworker
Had two family members
Executed sometime ago.
She has sadness in her
Eyes and I can relate.
She's in mourning
So am I…
I haven't had a drink in 5 days.

My God
The complications
The horrid complications of
Life and death and not being able
To vanish into a bottle
A sweet alcohol filled bottle.

I don't want to hear about
Children burning to death
Or executions
Or fucking, sleeping, defecating
Cars, or houses in neighborhoods
I can't walk through
Because my skin tone isn't right
Or sweet intoxicated prostitutes
Or suicide
Or ice cream trucks.

I don't want to contemplate
Reality or add 2 + 2
Think
Or hear of fellow citizens
I grew up with dieing
Blown to bits
In some Middle Eastern country.
Fuck no!
I haven't had a beer in 5 days.
That's the most important issue
I face right now.

The Babies Are Crying

The babies
Are crying
Because
They want
Milk.

After I get
A
Forty in me
I'll buy a gallon
For them
A
Whole gallon
Of milk.

After…
After I get
My
Forty.

Faggot

Someone told me
I shouldn't use the word
Faggot
In my poems.

He told me it would
Deter people from reading
My work.

I've never had anything
Against gay men or woman.
Never.
They're my brothers & sisters
Just as much as any.

When I use the word faggot
It's simply to show
The world
The extent of my fathers
Vocabulary.

Understand?

I was born
And named Joseph
But my father called
Me 'Faggot'.
He meant well, I guess.

So I tried to convene
This to the person
And he said:
Umm Humm!

Now I think
What will the homosexual
Community think of me?
My cousin gets along with me
And he's homosexual.

Well, I guess, time is too short
To fret over something
As a word
Being so offensive as to make
Grown men
Hate me.

And if they do hate me…
Well, I'd love to buy them a drink
And a dozen roses
And some chocolate
And maybe some sex toys
(I use them myself).

But as the world turns
And things being the way things
Are now…
My homosexual brothers & sisters
Will probably accept me

Much sooner then their
Heterosexual counterparts.

And like someone told me today
Only a truly illiterate person
Would fail to see
I mean no harm
When I write the word
Faggot in my work.

So with that said
I'll go out and have a smoke
Find a faggot
Sit and talk with him
And feel good
And laugh
And express to him
That I'm sure
Very soon
Someone will tell me I shouldn't
Use the word
Alcoholic
Either.

The Molded Man

I am born of mediocrity
And so I shall remain
Normal
So sensitive
Lost
Broken
Drunk bum on the concrete floor
Poet
Shattered
Cancer destined
However and whatever
Suits your
Individual.

Imagined Reality

Ahh, but then there's imagination
And a priceless imagination
Could substitute reality
For a moment or two.

Take me for example,
Myself.
Normal alcoholic with dreams
Of everything inside a bottle.
But…
I do desire.
There is a reality
I wish to know.

Myself,
I'd like to set up camp
On the cliff of a mountain
In the Himalayas
Or look for Itzamana
In an ancient Mayan ruin.

I'd like to know
The feeling of pressurization
And then exploration
Of the deepest Pacific
Depths.

I'd like to watch a sunrise
On an island in the Philippines
Home to the origin of my blood.

I'd like to have drinks with
Bukowski
Hemingway
Poe
Sexton
Naruda
Lorca
Ginsberg
& my grandfathers
In a bar somewhere
In northern England.

Or love without fear
Of loss.

Ahh, but then I'm just a normal
Sick bastard on a poem trip
Searching for God
With the tip
Of my
Pen.

My Body Is Toxic

My lungs swim in cigarette
Smoke & my stomach is
Filled with alcohol
And I have found my true form.

I had the beginnings of
Sickness
Sneeze
Cough
But sickness is formed by
Bacteria and my body is toxic.
No longer are these
Sickened signs
Evident.

My wife contracted ringworm.
Later, upon my flesh
I saw the makings of it.
And later still, upon my flesh,
I saw the death of it.
O how my flesh has been purified
By smoke & drink!

Wasted Potential?

I don't give a fuck about work
Anymore and don't remember
If I ever did.

Writing has enveloped me
And with it I have a sense
Of purpose the damned
Board of Education never once
Gave me or showed
Me or hinted fuckin' hinted
At me.
I don't want it
Anymore, if wanting it
Was ever an issue.

Vero doesn't think I have it
Doesn't believe in me.
There's always a mocking
In her tone when she talks
Of my work and
It's why I live.

I'm going to be thirty soon.
Five books under my belt.
I haven't wasted my
Potential.

Cigarettes & Drink &

Time will give me age
And with age
My body will brake

Fall into realms of uselessness.

"You got a light? Pass the pint!"

My lungs will die
My liver will perish &
When I am long dead
Someone will read this poem
And know that I wouldn't
Have had it
Any other way.

Gutter of Wonder

We see people and wonder what
Our lives would be like if…
But isn't that always the case
A deep yearning to know
Curiosity and all that jive?

I love the imagination so.
Without its conceptions of
Passion… drug use
Wouldn't be me lying
In the gutter with a bottle
In my hand.

I don't want wonder!
Hell no.
I want nothing to do
With wonder.
I'll stay right here,
In this gutter
With my bottle.

Infected With Poetry

We've been on some trip as of late.
It's certain... we almost lost
Each other on some sad note of
Despair. This one means that much!
It means that-that much to us!

She sat with me, trying to talk
Her talk. Familiar words spoken.
Demands of acceptance.
But I can't. I want more then
Us. I want more for my Isis.

What would it look like
Her teacher or friend or lover
Ask: "What did your Dad do
With his life?" She'd then answer:
"He was a broken dream."

Bukowski said it could mean
Losing everything. Lose-loss-pain
And I have to go all the way
I'm already committed.
I'm already infected with poetry.

She wants me to seek help
Even though I expressed my
Knowledge of poetry being

My therapy. She thinks the bottle
Is killing me.

I don't deny this.
The bottle. The writing.
It's all become obsession.
My hair has begun to fall out
And my migraines have returned.

It's been some trip as of late.
I realized unless I have a son
The name Padron will die with me,
That it will all end here
In this beautiful America.

Twisted And The Song Is In My Head

And I want to run free
Into the wilderness of glass
And concrete and dreams
Form on chaos
And television.

My love looks at me
With eyes of hatred
And I drink!
I drink like
The heavens have decided
To rain lager
And I gulp and slurp at
The possibilities
The dreams
The dreams
I am song and it's in my head
And I have tomorrow to work
Out the complications.

But here in this state
Of mind
All that truly matters is
How well I can face the
Minute.
How well I can hold sway

Over the terrible twisted
Song
Of myself and my dreams
And my alcohol.
How I love alcohol.

I will walk off into tomorrow
Walk off into some other
Song and hope
My drink carries me
Into the gift
Of forgetfulness.

O But I Have Not Shown You

O but I have not shown you
The true essence of my
Song
And the taste of life
God has so thankfully bestowed
Upon me
Wasted son of a broken man
I have seen my potential
And now
Now
I chase after it.

Breathing strong
Nostrils & lungs pumping
Heart ripping torrents of blood
Into my person
Love, I have not shown you
My truth
My essence
And how far you remain
From my soul
It's very unlikely
I shall ever come to terms with
Ever & ever showing you.

I fight into one direction
And you follow
Looking for purpose in my steps

Trying to make sense of it all
Like a
Man
Lost, tormented by mad desire
To follow in the footsteps of experience.

I do not intend to look back
When you fall
And if it should be me
That takes a dive…
If you should take sight of my
True form
I will weep for you

Because such burden
Will truly become
Your end.

Trust that!

Such Horror

A creature
Was captured last night
After being discovered.

His crime was vicious & disgusting.

This creature sexually
Abused countless children
Penetrating
Them in every imaginable way.

The say he was 58 years old

One of his victims was 8.

O great sadness of the world
I pray to the merciful lord
To withhold his mercy this
One single
Time
& give such pain to this creature
As to become legendary.

And if for some reason
This creature has
Innocence in his heart
And the accusations are false
May the good lord bless him

With health and strength
And the good sense
To leave
Forever behind
The sickness which can only
Be called

The Board of Education.

She Had

She had green eyes
And the way she smiled at me
And the way I felt
Inside…
But it's always the same
Always
Broken in such a way.

You step out of your home
And there she'll be
What should be
But what shouldn't.

I have a life already
So does she
We've only held the glimpse
Of each other a handful
Of times
But enough to last
Forever.

Will I question
What I am supposed
To be
Maybe for a second
Imagine how it could be?

No.

I have a beautiful wife
A beautiful daughter
And all my dreams
If ever
I
Had any
Have been fulfilled.

So when we see each other
Just the few minutes we share
Looking
Maybe imagining different endings
That's more then enough
At least
In
My
Case.

My Cousin

You call me in the early
Hours
Of night fall
And recite such powerful
Poetry
To me.

You ask my opinion
And I tell you the truth
I love it.

But your dreams
In words
Expect so much more then
A night of fine writing.

I wish I could tell you
That writing is the one thing
I hate in this world
But
Sadly I also have
The same amount of love
For it.

You must give your nights
Of sleep to it
Your love making sessions
Your ability to eat

None of it matters when
You're a writer.

My cousin
O how you will learn
Of its hardship
Sooner or
Later.

Devil In My Bedroom

Upon entering my place of sleep
Masturbation
Drunken essence of purity
I took sight
Of the Devil
Seated at my desk.

He was smoking a cigar
And working his cock
Up
And
Down.

"You're late." He says
moaning and spraying a load
of himself onto my
manuscript.
"There you go… I've blessed it!"

I blink

And he's gone.

The next morning
Upon my awakening
My manuscript is stained
And reeks of bad writing.
I move away from it

And catch hold
Of my breath.

My wife looks to me from
The bed
Half asleep
"What's wrong, Honey?"

"I've been blessed." I answer.

"That's good." She returns to her
sleeping position
and I say to her:

"No, Baby. It's not good."
And she doesn't see
When I scoop up
Every damned page
Of that blessed
Manuscript
And

Deposit it
In the
Trash.

"I'll start, again. Without any
blessing."

You Have Not Lost Me

You have not lost me
My sister.
I still live & love
I forgive and feel great regret
For your abandonment.

I do not hate you for it

I do not hate you
But
What is true is your pride
Has become such
A verdant force
In your meager life.

When I look to you
In my minds eye
I see myself.

When I look to you
In my heart
I see hopelessness
& tragedy.

Your soul has been corrupted
By the very creatures
You fought to escape.
You have become them

You have them in your eye
In your way
In your existence.

I weep for you.

I weep so much for you.

For where I have the love
Of your discarded family
And that of
My wife
My daughter…

You, my dear sister,
Have elected
A type
Of solitude
I can't help but admire.

And when death comes to me
Ready to take me into
A realm of chaos
I will look to my loved ones
And regret.

Upon your fall…
Regret shall remain
A long forgotten beast.

Two Raccoons

Two raccoons crossed
My path
And upon seeing me
They stopped
And stared.

Did I look as strange to them
As they did to me?

In this city of broken glass
And cigarette buds
How insane could it
Have been
To those two creatures
Seeing a man
On a porch in the middle
Of the night
Staring at them?

I exhaled smoke & they fled
Into the shadows
Of our urban madness.

They never looked back
Neither did I.

The Long Wait

My brother…
My sister…
What shall we do
With the lost dreams
We have accumulated?

Love them
Touch them
Fuck them

We go to work
Everyday with that routine
We find shelter
From the hardships

In lust
In smoke
In drink

And so patiently so very
Patiently
Wait for that moment
When we'll accept
Our death.

Useless

I am confused
Broken, forever
On some stone
In the middle
Of a burning
Forest.

I refuse to acknowledge
The lovers
Of my art

I refuse to acknowledge
The regulators
Of it

And
I am pushed
Aside
Useless.

Dry Trip

It has been
3 days
Since my last embrace
Of the bottle.

I am dry
The last Padron
On a dry trip
Trying
To face a world

Every predecessor
Of mine
Gave up on
Long
Ago.

A Real Hero

I once met a real hero
Long ago on a shore
Of childhood.
He told me his name
And he looked tall
Enough to touch the sky.

He wore a beard like Christ
And his hair was long
And black
And curly
And I would stare at him
In awe.

Everyone,
The people who loved him,
Called him
Stinky.

But he smelled of fine leather
And his hands
Felt of hard work.

He had a beautiful wife
And I loved his
Daughter
Like my own sister.

He worked in a shop
Fixing motorcycles
And I have a picture of
A day
As a child
In which he sat me atop
One of his road hogs.

One day,
Because there is a day for all of us,
Stinky
Was in the shop
Working to provide for his
Lovely family,
Fighting to make ends
Meet.

A boy ran into the shop
Screaming
That someone was trying to kill him.

Stinky
The warrior that he was
Told the boy to hide
Turned
And found a man standing behind him
Knife in his hand
And murder in his eye.

"It ain't goin' down like that, Brother."

Stinky
Protected the boy
And fought
The murderer.

He fought like a true man
He fought with love
And courage
And he could have done
What any other man
Would have

But he didn't.
He stood his ground
And never backed down.

There was a massive funeral
For him.
And I don't know what ever
Happened to the boy
He saved

But I think of him and
Wonder
If he realizes
A great man gave his life for his.

As a child
I met a hero once
His name was Stinky

He wore a black bandana
He smiled at me
He had dreams
And I will remember how
He stood
How he fought
How he believed in righteousness.

With his memory
Etched into my childhood
I will try
To be a better man

To look at my daughter
One day
And tell her
With tears in my eyes
That
Yes
I once knew a real live
Hero
That there was such a time
When
Heroes
Were real people.

Dry

I want to give up and I just
Don't want to – to; to take
This bullshit any more. I feel
Sick inside like death
Knows me and shit like that
My stomach feels dead and
My eyes are useless and
Immobile and I'm dry
Damn I'm dry I want
I want I want what
I can't have and I miss
It and my nerves are
Shattered fuckin' shattered.

My wife waits for me and I can't
Wait to see her touch her
Maybe gain strength within
Her presence.
No, not maybe!
I will and I will because
I believe it's so. Fordham
Will come soon and I will
Remember… my alcoholic
Brothers and the games of chess
We shared during the storms
And know that I wish to return
To the passion I felt there.
My drunken brothers of

Understanding. Whether
Broken with rage or grief
Or broken from the bottle
They understood me
Loved me.
Even me
A destitute creature
On a broken shore of
Concrete and lost… man, I'm
Lost.
Here in this sickening
Place known to so many
As reality… mine comes
In lager form.

I need to find my wife.
I'm dry.
I'm breaking.

God Speaks

A strong breeze
Opens my door.

It's God

Telling me
I must once again
Leave
My keyboard
To
Face the world.

To The Anti-Bukowski Publishers

Bukowski left as epitaph
On his tombstone
"Don't Try!"

In his writing he
Demanded
"If you're going to try
go all the way…"

I read Bukowski
And though I was too young
To appreciate him in his life
He has inspired
ME
To become something
I had given up
On.

I submit my poems to you
Dear publisher
And you say
"No more Bukowski wannabes!"

So I have written this poem to you
In the spirit of my great teacher
And I say:
"Fuck you! I won't stop!"

Together

We must stand together
Or the fall we'll suffer
Will be legendary.

We must stop the routine.
We must call to arms the sleeping multitudes.
We must love one another.
We must help the unfortunate.
We must pray for the forgotten.

We must stand together
With hands interlocked
And born as one.

We welcome death
Through sex
Through drugs
Through drink
Through violence
Through indifference
Through lack of originality
And acceptance of envy.

We must stand together
And fight for and end
To the chaos in our lives.

With lips of trust
We must kiss our siblings
Our parents
Our children
Our song of unity.

I will lose my life
Just as eventually
You will as well.
I will lose my feeling of word
Eventually
As you will lose your care
To read them.

But this is insignificant
To the full outcome
Of our tomorrow.

We must stand together
Or the likelihood
Of a tomorrow
Will become unlikely.

Or we can continue on as we have
As we always have
And remain
Useless.

Watermelon

I watch my daughter eating
Watermelon
And I remember sitting outside
Nonina's walk-in apartment
On a summer afternoon
Eating the same fruit.

She hadn't any teeth and the cold fruit
Felt fine between her old gums.

She would turn to me
And
Ask me if I liked the fruit
And always I'd say yes and the breeze
Would feel good across my
Bare arms & legs

I watch my daughter
Eating that fruit
Wishing we could have both
Sat beside Nonina
Wishing she could have
Experienced
How wonderful it felt sitting
Beside her great grandmother.

I take a slice, now, and a seat
Beside my child.

We eat the watermelon together
Father & daughter
And I tell her I love her
And hope
One day she'll look back and
Remember how it was to eat
Watermelon
With her
Daddy.

Fio

How I have seen struggle
In your attempt at life,
My sister!

How I have loved your passion
To be more then just ordinary
Woman born of effort
And hope.

You inspire me with this
Pride of yours & I feel
So much for you.
In your eyes I see
So much more than
You yourself could ever understand
And coming from me,
Your alcoholic brother,
It must be strange
To hear of your affect on
An insane poet.

You're not a bottle on my lips
But I love you all the same.

You kiss existence with hope
And fight each day with
Determination…
Determination that could

Make mountains shiver.
Your dreams may be
Unclear
To even your own self
But I see
Something so spectacular
In you.

I see strength
I see great endeavors
I see love
I see woman
I see dreams
I see fervor
I see what many have never
      Known of you.
I see a remarkable human being
That I am so proud to know.

In your face there are flashes of power
In your heart a beat of devotion
& your soul…

I've seen you once
Questioning yourself
And the path you have chosen.
Yes, I've seen you
On that long path into doubt.

But do not question yourself,
My sister,
Do not deter from what you
Are
Because if my eyes are correct
And my heart pure
And my soul poet

You are perfect more today
Then you have ever been
And shall ever be.

Now:
Hold your head high!
There's a poet
You inspire
And
He's your brother,
Your brother,
Forever.

Nailed

Nailed to the wall on Wednesday
I rose from the long dark slumber
With Christ on Sunday.

We shared a beer in laughter
And I loved him
And he loved me
And then
Before he confessed his hope
In my written word

He looked up into sky
And asked me:
"Do you believe in my Father?"

"My Lord… my faith is unwavering."
And he looked back at me
Smiled
And said:
"Then learn to forget my Father
and learn the ways of the wicked."

I did not reply to this
& he decided to continue.

"I want your suffering to become
a beacon in so your work
may speak truth through

Knowledge
And your knowledge will be
That any other way
But the way of my Father
Reigns forfeit."

And I walked away from my lord
Years ago and years ago
I learned what he wished of me.

How I long to return to that Wednesday
When we were together
And
I
Didn't feel so alone.

April 1, 2007

Woke
Smoked a cigarette
Wrote some poems
Smoked a cigarette
Wrote more poems
Smoked a cigarette
Went to the movies with my family
Smoked a cigarette
Visited Barnes & Nobles
Had coffee in Starbucks
Read some Bukowski
Met up with an old friend
Smoked a cigarette
Smoked a cigarette
Went to a restaurant in an SUV
  Filled with four children
  My mother in-law
  My wife
  My friend
  And my alcoholic self.
Smoked a cigarette
Ordered a burrito but didn't have a beer
  Things don't always go as planned
Smoked a cigarette
Bought some more cigarettes
Got diarrhea from the Starbucks coffee
Ate half of my burrito
Smoked a cigarette

Told Isis I love her
Came home
Smoked a cigarette in comfort on my porch
Shit in comfort in my bathroom
Watched some Discovery Channel
Smoked a cigarette
Called my cousin
Smoked a cigarette
Took a shower
Fucked
Smoked a cigarette
Wrote some poetry
Smoked a cigarette
Wrote some poetry
Wrote some more poetry
Smoked a cigarette
Read some Bukowski
Smoked a cigarette
Cousin called and as he recited his new
        Poem to me…
Smoked a cigarette
Drank a tall glass of cold milk
Looked at Isis asleep in my bed
Pissed
Listened to some music
Wrote poetry
Smoked a cigarette
Shit, again
Decided to go to sleep
        Right after I indulge

>   In one more cigarette
>   Just one more
> Prayed to God
> Picked Isis up and carried her to her bed
> Found comfort in the darkness
> And came to terms
> That it hadn't been a bad day
>   After all,
>   I had cut down the smoking
>   To only what was
>   Absolutely
>   Necessary.

A Poem To My Past

Fuck you, Past!
The beatings
The cursing
The dog walking
The dreaming
The praying
The masturbating
The insomnia
The homelessness
The drugs
The bottle
The loneliness
The screaming
The suicide attempts
The cold nights on park benches
The death of my aunt
The death of my grandmother
The damned routine job
Some more of the bottle
      For a several more years
The fear of tomorrow
I ain't never
Ever
Going back
To a damned second of any
Of that shit
Ever again…ever, ever, ever!
Well… maybe the bottle.

I Have Inspired

I have inspired
And touched with love
The lost and forgotten.

It was my CHOICE.

I could have accepted
My uselessness but no…
Such a fall is tasteless
Meaningless & boring.

Really,
What more could a person
Ever hope to accomplish
Then that as a gift
Of inspiration

And I have inspired.

Memory of my self
Shall remain in the thoughts
Of countless
And I will love them
As a father loves his children
As a mother loves
The flesh she births.

And I have inspired.

Alcoholic on sheets of life
Abused child and
Drug addicted teenager
I have given freely
What no one found fit
To give me.

And I have inspired.

With shaking hand
Tortured sense of mind
My daughter shall see
Father as addict
Addicted to strong drink
And hope
And when I fall
(which is often)
It's on purpose
& I find my purpose
With pain and struggle
And my words have
Shown this.

O how I have inspired.

I have driven the illiterate
To the page & the pen.
The repressed have
Given their children

Understanding
With their written word.

And I watched them
Loved them all
And wrote to them
Of them through them.
I have not squandered
My gift.

I use it well
I give it willingly.

And I smile… still praying
To one day find
A release from my moments
Of deep depression.

And with my death I shall inspire.

My daughter on song
I hope and pray for
Your soul
For you were born of me
And have the gift I have.

May you find peace, my little love.
A peace in art
I never knew.

Sooner Or Later

I saw a raven this morning
Flying through the dark murk
Of early mourning hour.

He perched upon a tree branch
And looked down at me
Silent.

"What's up, Brother?"

No answer.

And then I thought of Poe.
Poe and his greatness,
His terrible alcoholism.

"Hey, tell Poe I'll catch up to him
sooner or later."

The raven cawed,
Took flight & vanished
Into the sea of branches
On Pelham Parkway…
Fleeing from the rising
Sun.

They're So Many

They're so many hidden
Realities in this wretched
World. Constantly changing
Turning
Becoming adapt to the
Next and next victim.

My good friend
Here are my words
This…
The page
The written scheme.

This… my truth, my form
My reality
For all to see
And judge freely.
I accept my persecution.

I'd rather my soul lay bare
Than hidden behind
A lying truth.

Fine Quality Paper

Envelope after envelope
I submit my work
To the world and the world
Returns to me
Rejection
On the finest quality paper.

Water marked.
The most appealing textures.
Personally I have grown
Quite fond of the papers beauty
That I now laminate them
Preserving there influence
Upon me.

The ink is too precious
To set free into the elements
Of time.
Such fantastic type!
"We regret to inform…"
And I'm left humbled
By the power of that
Type.

So now in my hand
I possess the next two
Submissions.

Soon I will have two more
Gorgeous rejections to lust over.

I can't wait.

Well-Up

The weather is warming
People are relaxing
I've slowed my drinking
And resumed
My smoking.

Bukowski advised
I not push my poetry.
Let it flow.
When it's welled-up
To such a point
That great God
Himself wouldn't
Dare hold it back.

He didn't say this
With these words
But nonetheless
This is what I interpreted.

Thankfully my hand
Is still good
And my mind
Works well enough.

Not how I would want it
But well enough.

O How The World Has Left Me

O how the world has left me
This broken man with
Untouchable dreams
Accumulated during sad
Moments of existence.

The tears don't help
Anymore…
Neither love.

The bottle is my only remedy
To the loneliness.
The bottle and the solitude
It provides me,
The blessed one dimensional
Solitude.

Looking back
The scarred remnants
Of childhood
Burdens unleashed
On a sofa of death.

Empty shell casings
Winchester primers
And the God awful
Bags of black powder.

How many rounds
Did I help make?
How many men did I help
Kill?

There's no redemption
For a man like me.
No calm without…
Without the bottle.

Tonight I will look towards the stars
And pray for
Forgiveness.

Endangered Species

Most of my Philippine family
Were killed off during WWII.
Now,
So many years later
We face extinction.

I look at those
That remain
And I feel it in my heart…
The end.

It was a great run.

My Filipino relatives
Warred with the Japanese
And fell.
The great warriors of my bloodline.

My Italian blood
Across the vast Atlantic
Doesn't recognize us.
The tainted black-sheep American
Relatives.

My Puerto Rican blood
Fell to the bottle,
The smoke & the ass.

Their extinction
Has long been told.

It was a great run.

Holding my daughters hand
I look to a future
That may see a new
Beginning.

Holding my daughters hand
Watching her smile
I will remain her soul image…
The key to a vicious past…
The last of her bloodline.

She will know of her origin.
The warriors and drunkards
Alike.

And when she becomes the head
Of her own family
She will look back at us
And our respectable trials

And have all the answers.

Arthur

I began my return to chess
With the insistence of an old man
Named Arthur.

We played countless games
Down in the Aqueducts.

& it was good.

There were other players
But it didn't matter…
They didn't matter.
We played like brothers
Born of different times
And united with 64 squares.

& it was good.

Cigarette smoke
And laughter.
Man, I didn't want to play
Chess ever-ever again.
But that old man…
He brought it all out of me.

When he left,
Retirement somewhere in Florida,
I returned to our table

And
Others sat in his stead
But it wasn't good
And soon…
Soon I left the Aqueducts.

& it was good.

I Am Chaos

Sifting / sifting – sifting
Through the madness.
I am chaos
The ravage sifted into
A bottle
Of chaos.

They say be original.
Fucking tragic misery.
Hammers through faces.
Ripped-off finger nails.
I've given my toxic body
My liver
My lungs
To the multitudes
& now I am legion
On a carpet of damnation,
Through a gate of
Tremendous fire
& nauseating brimstone.

I shall pollute the page
With FUCK YOU
Fuck you / Phuck you
Fuk u
And in the end & across
The heavens they will
Regret their fallen son.

The Ass Is Out

The weather is beautiful now
& the ass is out
Hangin'
Out skin tight jeans
Singing 'bout come 'Fuck me!'
And youth is so straight
Forward & visible.

These women run amuck
And I pity their sexual
Desire.
Disease and childbirth
Is all they'll find
And then… then
The next generation
Will be known
Because all that had
To be known
Was shown before
Their birth.

Such a terrible pity.

Whatever I see
I shall wipe from my mind
And continue
On.

Sometimes Late At Night

Sometimes late at night
I still feel I can call her
Speak to her on the phone.
Tell her something simple
Something pure
Like
"I love you."

The way she held me as a child
& sheltered me as a man.

She's been gone so long, now.
And life has bee so gruesome
Since.

Next time I won't take
Those 'I love you's'
For granted.

You Push Them Aside

You push them aside

Though they tell you
Confess to you
On their knees
Their love for you.

You push them aside.

They offer you shelter
Money, food, dreams,
Light, stars, a hug,
But it doesn't matter.

You push them aside.

When they seek you out
Ask of your well being
Show concern
Attachment
"Fuck them!" you say.

You push them aside.

They don't matter.
They're apart of a past
You want nothing of.

Memories
God-damned included.

You push them aside.

Then, when life for you
Couldn't be better.
Fortune giving you
Every dream you've
Ever conceived.

You push them aside.

And as years go by
Days without their
Constant badgering
Of love and how they'd
Have sacrificed for you.

You push them aside.

Now the solitude
You fought for is all yours
And their badgering
Is over
And the storm has passed.

You push them,
Push them,
Push them aside.

Then the phone call.
Death has rung home
And you're forever alone.
They're gone
Into some other realm.

They've left you here alone.

And you're resentful
So resentful of their
Abandonment.

Tomorrow, when you look in the
Mirror, that cold
Reflection staring at you…

Push that shit aside

Because it's what
Matters most.

Voyage

Voyage into the routine
The same old – same old
Wake shower shit
Dress smoke bus
Work bus home
Wake shower shit
Dress smoke bus
Work bus home
Etc & etc…
And the cycle is forever
And ever and my soul
Abandoned originality
Long-long ago.
Now-now all that
Remains is some sick
Type of echo,
A broken, forever
On a veneer of
Omega
Forgotten
And the sun rises
Into nothing…
Nothing at all.

The Cats

The cats are out

The cats are out wondering
The city night.
Hiding beneath parked cars
Searching
Garbage pails for shelter.

They hike their skirts up
For the world to see
Their power
Spread their odor
On the laps of paying men.

The cats are out

Fucking in the shadows
And purring in echoes.

Tails lifted high
Ass bare for the multitudes
They seek out penetration
And deliverance.

They scamper across the night
Scene
Looking for highs or downs

Pissing on the faces of
Horny suckers.

The cats are out

Trooping by with their legs
Immaculate and untouchable
Pleading
With me to satisfy.

And will I?

Hell,
You can be sure
A dog like me
Is locking his door
Tonight.

They Tell Me

They tell me
That my language
The language of my poetry
Is terrible.

They say I curse too much
And that isn't acceptable
In the literal world.

Ahhh,
Like my father used to say
"Fuck'em all!"

They can't truly expect a man of art
To produce the greatest art
By placing restrictions on his art.
I'll write MY words how I deem fit
And if I want to use words like:

Dick, dickhead, faggot, pussy, cunt, muff-muncher,
cock-sucker, lesbian, bull-dagger, shit, shit-head,
muthafucka, asshole, dildo, whore, bitch, & etc…

That's my choice & to hell
With whomever doesn't agree
With free speech.

I've Started

I've started drinking
Again
And though I hate myself
Whole heartedly for it
I feel as if it's the
Right thing to do
(words of an addict).
Damn it all
I just want
Peace.

Consideration

I've considered being
And
Found that yes,
I am a being.

I've considered nothingness
And
Found that yes
There's nothing
In nothingness.

Sartre had some greatness
In his words and I have
Enjoyed his work
But
There's always that
Sense of lost time
When reading
Philosophy.

I get the same thing
From Nietzsche…
Something like Blah-Blah-Blah-Blah.

Marx & Engels
Bored me half to death
With their Manifesto.

Dostoevsky never
Let me down in way
Of an interesting read.
His *Idiot* was one great work
Not to mention
Demons.

Palahniuk,
That modern genius,
Has always come through
With originality
& flare.

But then
Dostoevsky & Palahniuk
Wrote and write fiction.

While Sartre and Nietzsche
Marx & Engels
Wrote philosophy.

I'm staying clear of both
Genres.

I'll remain a poet and keep
The title
'Bukowski Wannabe!'
O how it has such an attractive
Ring
To it.

Jungle

Went into the city with my family
Today and it was fantastic.

While on the train
Isis had to pee so we
Quickly
Strapped a diaper onto her little bottom
And told her to make pee-pee.

She said no and her tiny lips
Curled into sadness as she confessed
Her desire to hold it in.
She was so strong in her
Reserve
But fell to the burning force in her
Lower belly soon after
And the pee pushed through
Her diaper and
Darkened her jeans.

She started to say sorry
And looked at my mother-in-law.

I carried her most of the day
Through the hordes of city dwellers
And shoppers and beggars, shit-heads
Cock-suckers, half naked women, and drunks.

It was great.

She sat atop my shoulders
And I pushed through the madness
Into thrift shops and mega-stores,
Restaurants and across streets.

Throughout it all
I thought I'd rather my daughters
Pissed pants
Upon my neck, the weight
Of her body pushing me into
The concrete

Then a moment alone
In this treacherous city
And I stood straighter
Felt stronger
And smiled at the love I carried,
The love I call
My
Daughter.

Sloth

Some of us
Dwell
So
Deeply
Into our
Dreams
That we forget
To
Live.

Regression

I'm not supposed
To be here!
Where I am right now
Is what I left
Behind
So many months ago.

And here I am,
Again.

I remember how much
I loved it, feeling it.
This sort of feeling…
I felt it nowhere else
& it's good.
So tainted
Like
All that matters
Is now
And right now
All I want is calm.

This is bad!
I must stop before
I fall again…
Again.

Tremendous

A tremendous depression
Has set in motion
A burning pain
Deep within my fucking
Heart.

The cigarette smoke
Bathes over my face
And the rain
Those April showers
Have me longing
For May.

A man parked his car
In front of my house
As I stood on my porch
Smoking
And giving my self to the elements.

He looked at me
And smiled as if he
Could ever understand
Why I would brave the world
With a single cigarette
In my hand.
His stride was that of calm
And I would have
Sent my foot up his ass

If it hadn't been
For the Bukowski book
In my hand
And the fear of rain destroying
The pages.

O, but to hell
With the madness
And the depression.

I have poems swimming inside
My soul
Waiting to meet the page.

With a beer in hand
I'll embrace the burning pain in my chest
And try
To make sense
Of
It
All.

Why Even…

Why even try to fight
What can't be fought.
It's like death
And we're trying to flee
From it and there's
No god-damned
Escape.
The sun lies to us
With something like hope
Shining in our eyes
But it lies
It lies
And after the drink
Has worn off
And the nicotine
No longer matters
Staring in the mirror
I can see the lie
There behind my eyes
Like a dead dog
Asking for a burial
In a field of shit filled
Diapers from the
Young & old
Alike.
My fingers feel numb
And Bob Marley
Tries his best

To tell me of revolution
And to stand for something
But if he were alive
I'd tell
Him to stop lying to me
Because
Revolution for what?
There's nothing worth
Revolting
Over.
Trust me, I'd say.
I've tried tasting
Purpose
And all I've ever found
Were frozen Popsicles
Of shit
Moist for the licking.
My cousin got fucked up
On some good shit
Like this Popsicle I speak of
And when I asked him if
He had been able
To write anything
He said no
He said he had gone beyond
Writing
And I envied him.
I have never gone beyond
Writing.
Even with the stale

Taste of lager on my tongue
In my mouth
I haven't a clue as to
What
Beyond even means.
Once I forgot to get out of bed
To go piss
And I was left
Half asleep
In soaked sheets of
Liberation.
Pissing myself had given me
A freedom I had
Forgotten way back
In my infancy
&
Now Bob Marley
Doesn't make sense anymore
Maybe
I'll walk away from
This keyboard
Go back to the bathroom
And force myself
To throw-up
The little fight
I have left
Floating around inside
My belly.

Nicky

Was the new kid in class
And he got the run of it
Back then
I was nine years old
And had already
Made my reputation
As a good
Fighter
Nasty but damned good
In a brawl.

He didn't speak a hint of
English
And communicated
In Yugoslavian or Albanian
And
It was that first day
After school
When the predators
Decided poor Nicky
Was gonna get it.

As I was walking home
That day
Through the park
I saw two boys
Tearing Nicky apart.

One was choking him
While the other
Was sending
Blow after blow
Into Nicky's chest.

I acted quick
Realized that one of the
Assailants had taken
A great beating from me
Months before
And sent my book bag
Down hard into the kid
I didn't know.
He fell
And the boy choking
Nicky, the boy who had tasted
My fighting,
Let Nicky go and started
To flee,
His friend followed.

After that
It was some time before
Nicky left my side.

All the way to High School
When we went our separate
Ways
Nicky was my friend.

After a ten year gap
I ran into Nicky
In an arcade in Manhattan
And we hugged.

"Carlos!" he started. "How you doin' my brotha?"

I said fine…

"Listen," He continued. "I have a business now
And I want you to have a taste.
It's for free, my brotha.
It's for old times."
A beautiful young woman
Came into view
And it was then that I realized
Nicky was a pimp.

I declined and introduced him
To my wife.

After that night
I never saw
Nicky again.

For Your Self

My brother writes the most
Truthful poetry.
His words jump out of the page
And rip reality
Into the consciousness
Of everyone lucky enough
To have actually understood
His words.
His words are like falling rain drops
In a desert that
Sees rain drops only once a decade.

The other night
After reciting to each other
I asked him
Why is it he fears being published
And
He answered me with:

"I don't want to be rejected, Carlos."

So I say: "And how do you feel
After you've written a poem?"

"Like everything's going to be alright."

So as we walked through the night
Continuing our recitals

And loving the words we
Were sharing
I began to question my self.

If such a great poet
Were to die and the world
Never managed to accept his words
Who would be at loss?
The world or the poet?

But then none of that stuff mattered
Then and it doesn't matter
Now.

I'll be content with my rejections
Pray to God
Hope He hears me
Drink as much as I can
Smoke more then I can
And write
Not for the world
But
For my self.

Bullshit

An old man living
Next door to me
Has been spreading the word
That the writer
Next door to him
Is always out on his porch smoking
And smoking
And it seems like all the writer
Knows how to do
Is smoke.

I grew angered
Upon first hearing this
But then
It tapered off into something
Like constipation
And nausea.

What does it matter what that
Old buzzard
Thinks of me just as long
As he has gotten the one aspect
I truly care for correct.

You see,
During the entire time he spoke of me
He called me the
writer

& if I smoke
And appear to be cancer-ridden
So be it…
I'm a writer in his
God-damned old eyes.

The next time I saw him
Walking his dog on my sidewalk
I was exhaling
What I would call a great
Massive exhale.

He looked at me and I said:
"Hey, how you doin', Old timer?"
He answered with a "Fine. And you?"

And I inhaled what I would
Like to call a
Great massive inhale
And said:

"Working on my next book."

"O really!" His dog started to shit
On my sidewalk. "What in the world
Could it be about?"

A great massive exhale.

"It's about elderly people

And the fact that nothing
Gets by them."

He wished me luck
And ever since then
I call him 'Old Timer'
And try to make sure
That when
We cross paths
There's a cigarette in my hand
Or
Mouth.

Playing At God

My 6th grade teacher once sat
With me and complimented
Me on a short story I had
Turned into her.
She praised me and said
I had surprised her with my ability
To tell a story.

Looking down at the pages
In her hand
And the giant red 'A+' on the cover
I thought
This was the start of something
Great and beautiful and real
And then she asked me
The question that has
Haunted me during the few moments
I actually
Manage to write fiction.

"Why do you write, Carlos?"

Thinking, then, of my father
And how he cursed me
And all the times I killed him on paper
I answered:

"I write because I can do what I want

on the paper
and… I like being God."

She smiled and I smelled
Coffee
On her breath.

"One day you're going to be
a great writer, Carlos. Don't ever give
up."

And I had my first fan.

She never expected anything from me
Other then a new story
Every two or three days
And I wrote them and was excluded from
Doing homework, class work, consciousness
During class hours, and participation.

Looking back
I wonder if she
Really knew how much
I loved writing
Those stories
For
Her?

Getting Married

She's damn near forty years
Old
Talking abut marrying a man
She hardly knows.

I'm twelve years younger
Act twice as mature
Work much harder
Sleep a lot less
Have a child & she's childless
Drink every chance I get
Smoke continuously throughout any given day
Wash my own clothes
Find time to write
& have been married for a cool
      Ten years, now.

She still has her family cater
To her every beck & whim.
She claims to have known the
Groom to be for a very long time
But when she looks at me
It's there
In her sad face
And I can't help but wonder
If a long time for her
Was last night.

She can seek out
What she cares to seek out
And when she discovers
The fighting
The terrible arguments
The disagreements
Or what ever the hell
I'll stand there
A week after the marriage
With my beer in my hand and smoke
Clouds above my head
And ask:

"When's the divorce?
It's gonna be awesome and frankly
It's been a long time coming."

My Sister

Wants me to tell her
How I feel
So she can have a reason to hate
Me.

I refuse to even hint
At my drunken emotions!?
I write this poem sober
And dry and say "Yeah, that's right, I love you!"
Hoping she can decipher
The hidden message behind
Sober & drunken.

It'd be easy to give in to anger
And rage,
Disappointment

And "Fuck you! I hope you shit blood!"

But then I've never been
One for the easy road
& she's never been one
To look behind
The
Words.

Reading At Night

I read some Buk for
A few hours today
While I had
Absolutely nothing
To do.

In one of the poems
I read
He wrote of other poets
Being angered
At his fame
And I thought
Here is one of the greatest
Poets to have ever walked
The face
Of this
World
Writing of envy.

What would the world
Do with another
Chinowski?
Weep?
Celebrate?

He wrote that the
Young poets
Were looking to dethrone

Him
And I couldn't help but smile
At that page
Because
The legacy he has built
Can never be matched
Imitated
But never matched.

Old man,
Hank,
Chinowski
Buk
Don't you worry your genius
Up there in the stars,
Brother.
You've inspired entire
Generations
To pick up and
Try to do
And don't.

I won't comment on
How great you were
But
You had something special
And I've been chasing it
Ever since
'Factotum.'

Brother.
I wouldn't have
Thrown beer cans at your
Window at night
Screaming for your recognition
But I sure as hell
Would have had
A few
With you in the
Bar.

Prepared

Some envelopes today
This morning
While the damned dog
Next door
Barked at nothing
Absolutely nothing
At all.

I started to feel like
The Son of Sam
With that damned dog
Yapping all damned day.
I write
Now only because
It's two in the morning
And the damned thing is asleep
Somewhere
Out there.

Yap!
And I told my wife
To get the poison ready
I had to kill something
But she
Refused
And that bastard
Kept right on yapping.

I went out for a few
To smoke a cigarette
And the damned thing
Started up
As soon as he saw me.

Amazing! I thought.

Looking at him I began
To tell him of my plans
& he stood silent
listening:

"I'm gonna go get my hammer
up stairs, little fella. And then I'm
going to sink it
right smack dab in
the middle of your
beautiful eyes!"

He started yapping.

"Yeah, I'm going to take my time
killing you."

And then the little bastard
As if he understood
Took off
Leaving a trail of dust
In his retreat.

Pinky

Long ago I snubbed my pinky toe
On the door frame
And kneeling in pain
I vowed to
Cut that little fucker
Off one day.

I have a sharp pair
Of scissors aching for the task
But I refrain
Only because
I haven't time
To recuperate from
Such a deliverance.

Upset

The story is always the same
And the same story
Always has terrible written
All over it
Pores seep the nonsense
Of it
And here I am
Trying my hardest
To switch up a bit.

I think now
That the world has changed so much
That change has become
The standard.

I read such madness
From the so called masters
Of modern lit
That when I pick up
A Dostoevsky
Or flip through some Sexton
Or have an unforgettable
Evening with Chinaski
I feel
So appreciative
Of their respectable
Influences upon me.

The night is long and
The page isn't blank
I'm appreciative
Of
This.

The story is mine
And whether or not it changes
Depends solely
Upon my
Decision,
My choice.

Goose Flesh

My wife massages me
By pulling at
The hair on my arms
And lower back
And the goose
Flesh
Pocks up on my
Body entire.

She really knows
How to make me feel so great
Comfortable
You relax the way
I relax
And it feels x-rated
Or illegal,
Unnatural.

She takes care of me
Always & I love her for caring
For me so
I love her for those fingers
Working my
Aching flesh away.

She smiles now
After so many years
Together

And simply pulls my hair,
Makes me feel like a million
Dollars,
Like the days are priceless
And the goose flesh
Fascinating.

Age And I'm Fast Approaching

It's been a long time
A great hand at the table
&
Now we must divvy up.

There is nothing so satisfying
Then the knowledge
Of end
And the expectation of
It.

We could lie to ourselves
Lie to the world
Hope for belief
But the ante has been wagered
And the end is fast
Approaching.

The shit has been pushed aside
The drink has been drank
The smoke smoked

We haven't
But a moment
And
Indeed
it's been such a great
Moment.

We lost our lives
For a second
Our body
Numb with toxin
And it was how age
Should have been.

When the great lord
Whoever he may be
Stands
Ready to judge
Us
Ready to collect his debt

We'll ask for
A little credit
And
A second chance at it.

Text Messaged

It's Easter
And the city is silent
The families are together
Toasting to another year
Treasuring their lives
Alive
Humbled
Happy.

My phone vibrates
As I watch the sky
Darkened by night,
Vast in my sight.
I exhale my cigarette
Smoke
And look at the phones
LCD screen.

It's been so long
Since I've even heard
From my sister
And there
On that LCD
It reads I have a new message

Not new
No
It's always the same for her

She rids her life
Of love
And compassion
Friends & family
And then a text message.

"Happy Easter!"

I inhale a deep drag
Hold onto it a moment
Release
Freedom and sense of mind
Flaring in gray cloud
Across my face
Put the phone in my pocket

And say aloud
Up to the stars
"Happy Easter to you, too!"
And I pray where
Ever she is
Either alone or with a friend
She hears me.

Yes...I Want To

My wife asked me to come to bed
And sleep beside her.
O how I wanted to listen,
Heed her words

The dogs are running the street
The bats have taken over
The skies
And I have a disease
That won't allow me to rest
Peacefully.

I am a poet.

It's damned hard being this
Treacherous lying creature.
Hard work
Damned hard work
Sitting here and writing
Trying to make sense of the nonsense
Trying to fight it without
My bottle.

So I sit here
In the murk
Spirits circling me questioning
My desire, asking me
If I think it's worth it.

What words can I give
That they don't already know?

I don't have the luxury
Of time
The luxury of money
The luxury of dreams
I don't have eternity to muse
Over my situation
The situation of myself

The world is too grand a place
To indulge in my self
Too grand a place.

She does look so beautiful
There
Sleeping with our daughter in her
Arms. They look good…
Like a pardon in front of
A firing squad.

The light seeps in from the street
It rips open my mind and
Torments me. Her voice
And yes… I want to

I want to join you
But there's work to be done, my love
Words to be written.

Curse Me, My Beauty

Versatile
The waters sway to & fro
Curses thrown in my direction
And I'm the catcher behind
The plate
I'm the shit-heel
Keeping your balance.

Do you remember
How I left
My life for a moment
Leapt into a taxi
And rescued you?

Alcoholic that I am
You called me
For help
When all I had to give was my time
Didn't even need to
Give me a 'thank you!'
Remember that?

Nah! It's all irrelevant.
With you it's always been
Irrelevant.

My beauty
You're like an empty beer can

With a long night
Ahead
And not a cent to my name.

The next time
You want to curse me
That urge boiling up out of your belly
& into your mouth
Take a second
And know
That
That shit is just gonna roll right off of
Me
And back onto
You…

I'll
      Make
            Sure
                  Of
                        It!

Explicit

"Faggot!" He called me.

F
Fu Fu
Fuc Fuc
Fuck Fuck
Fuck y Fuck y
Fuck yo Fuck yo
Fuck you Fuck you
Fuck yo Fuck yo
Fuck y Fuck y
Fuck Fuck
Fuck

A tear drop to cast
All those doubts away
There, there, my child…
Get it all out
And I guarantee
You'll feel much better.

And he held me close
Enough to hear his
Heart
And I hated him more.
I hated him so much more.

Vonnegut Dead At 84

I read Slaughterhouse Five
Five times
Read Cat's Cradle
Three times
And
Kurt taught me that you
Didn't have to have a bachelor
Degree
In order to follow
Your dream.

He was one of my first teachers
And I was a student of his word.
I learned
Of the short chapter
And
With his words
I enhanced my ability to
Imagine.

He taught me well.

And when my childhood
Tore holes through
My soul
Kurt was there in my hands
Telling my about *Ice-Nine*.

I will miss
The great talent
Of this modern master.
More & more
It
Seems
The great writers fade
Away leaving
No one at all to take their
Place.

Ahh, but we have his 21 books
And dear
Kurt shall
Live through
Them
Forever.

Fall Again

I am not supposed
To be here!
Where I am right now
Is what I left
Behind
So many months ago

And here I am
Again.

I remember how much
I loved it, feeling it.
This sort of feeling…
I've felt it nowhere else.

It's so good,
So tainted
Like
All that matters
Is now
And right now
All I want is calm.

This
I know is bad
& I must stop before
I fall again…
Again.

Every Step Forward

Every step forward
Feels like a step backward.

Today I'll rest
Tomorrow too
& Sunday
I'll write.

I need time to clear
My head of all the distractions
&
Fill it with what's
Important.

Bane Of Existence

I look back now
Towards yesterday
And
As much as I want
To hate myself
I can't.

I tell myself
That it's wrong & then
It happens.

To hate & love ones
Self…
To know one's self
Is the bane of existence.

I try to destroy myself
Without restraint and I
Care too little for those
Around me.

Selfish?

Yes, that's what I am.

Selfish!

And as they look upon me
Covered in their
Veils
Caring for me

I will accept the consequences
The trials
& tribulations
With a beer
In one
And a smoke
In the other.

I Walk Myself Into Pain

I
Walk myself into pain,
Into this
I
Call Gods name in vain
Lookin' for bliss
Pick up my pen…
Write down my
Life
Then that voice like a drill
Comin' from my wife
Tellin' me to stop
What I've become
Wake,
Begin to hope
& listen to my souls
Conceptual
Drum.

But
I can't because I've fallen
I
Read this poem
And know I am
Broken.

Princess

"What would you like today?"
I asked with a drunken smile
Across my face.
"I've got pizza and cheese burgers."

The child stood
At the cafeteria window
Staring at me as if I were
Some type of weird space alien
Straight
Out of the Twilight Zone.

"Come on, Girl!" What do you want?"

She was about nine years old
& one could see in her youth
A beauty that was unmarred
By life
& complete
& total innocence.

So I provided her
With a dose of reality.

"Pickup some food & get
out of my window, NOW!"
She did as told with tears
Welling in her eyes

"I've got other kids to feed
for Christ sake. Princess
or not, move along!"

The next day
She took her tray
Without a hint of hesitation
And I smiled.

She had learned so quickly.

Smile

Ask me if I hate you, father.

In the eyes of child
Father is the sole image
Of what God is supposed to be.

If your father
Claims you to be
A worthless piece of shit
And he wishes he could have
Persuaded his wife to have
Had an abortion,

How the fucking hell
Are we to view
That damned
Image
Of
God?

With a smile?

Ask me if I hate you, father
And I'll give you a smile
Satellites across the galaxy
Will envy.

Poet

I am greatness
The screaming flame
The saddened song
The words that make tomorrow.

Working In A Cafeteria Full Of Children

New York City
The Board of Education
Here
There's no time to think
Here
There's not much time
For anything
But
The screaming children.

SCREAMING

Screaming all day
Through every single hour.
Luckily,
Unlike my thoughts,
I have gotten used to the shouting.
My brains
&
Ears are dead
But, I'll be alright.

The Reason

You're the reason
They aren't killing me
Father.

When I feel weak
Broken
& torn apart by
This cruel world
I remember your lessons
In toleration.

The torturous words
The knowledge of weaponry
The virtuous aspects
      Towards life.

You're the reason
They aren't killing me
Father.

The government has stripped me
Of any and all dignity
I could have ever hoped to attain
In my wretched life.

Strong drink & smoke
Pollute my body, my flesh
And the trees look dead

And the stars don't shine
But…

You're the reason
They aren't killing me
Father.

When you put a gun
In my hand and declared
I take my own life
If I hated life
So god-damned much…

When you broke my face
With your fist & left
My manhood bloodied
Tarnished with a lack
Of will and dreams…

You're the reason
The aren't killing me
Father.

So whether it's heard
Or read one hundred years
From now… in a bathroom
Or the halls of the Vatican
Across the face of the oceans
Or atop of the cliffs of mountains
At the gates of hell

Or the realms of heaven.

Thank-you.

Lost Souls

Last night we wondered
The city
Saw a movie
Talked of our lost loved ones
Smoke & drank our
Sadness away
For a moment it was good
And the memories were
Pure
Flowing
Sensible.

Needed Time Together

We were finally going
To have some alone time
Together.

She had scheduled
A trip to Atlantic City
Some gambling
Some smoking
Though she never smoked
Some drinking
Though she never drank
And us
Us & us being together
And it would have been great,
Great indeed.

But the weather was
A bit on the
Terrible side
And the morning cup of coffee
Bitter like
Age.

In the diner
Before departure we had
Buttered rolls.
I smoked afterward
And we looked

Forward
To being together.

But the weather was frigid
And in our hearts,
Though it felt great
To be together,
Our hearts
Our damned hearts…

Our daughter was home
Without us and in bed
And deep inside
We had to face the facts:
It wasn't just we two
It was now we three.

We cancelled our trip
Made our way back home
Looked down at our
Sleeping daughter
And felt
Then
We were complete.

Granda-Padron, The Simpleton

They want…
They want…
I've given my ass
Entire
But, still they want
& I no longer have.

I'm too simple
They say
What they want
Is remarkable dream-
Like words
In forms of bliss
They cannot produce
Themselves.

This is what
They want.

They say they've
Already assumed my conclusion…
That all they have
To know
Of me is evident
And that's
That.

What a way
To shit on a man.

My fellow poets
Praise me
Praise my work
As if my dreams
Their dreams had been
Made clear.

"The simpleton can do it…
Why can't we?"

And then they praise
My poet and poetess
Family members
See this
Read this
Feel this
Light in me.

But then the others
- those that matter -
Have passed
Their judgment of me
Have given me the title
Wannabe & imitation.

It's funny how those
Who lack artistic inclination

Are so dreadfully quick
To judge those who
Have embraced artistic talent.

It's as if envy were a full time
Art
As well.

Routine Of The Scheme

The vacation is almost over
Soon I'll have to work
Again
Bust my hump…
Return to slavery…

I don't like it
I don't like it one bit
The scheme
The entire scheme
Is treacherous,
Broken.

My wife
She tells me to find
Another job
Better work
Another dream to drink away
"But," I say. "God has given me
a gift
and I'll be damned
if I waste it."

So I write the poems
And they keep coming
Out
Of
Me

Corrupted & polluted
O how the routine of the scheme
Has broken me

& my vacation is dead
The dogs will yelp
The cats will be run over
& the children will be fed.

But I don't like it.
For Christ sake
I don't like it.

It's some damned struggle
We have to face.

Look at my hands
At your hands…
Aren't they as bloody as our souls?

Yeah, say it!
I have.
"Fuck it all!"

A Choice

So long to the whatever
So long and it was
Now or never.
So long to the sounds
Of passion
So long to the words
Of fashion.

I choose the barbaric
A return to once was.
I choose the simplistic
A choice of love.

Given All

Now
What are we to do
When we've tried…
Given all we have
Life included
Time lost
Our death toll numbered?

What in the hell
Shall we do with what
Has been forgotten…
What we never wanted
To let go?

Buk said "Don't try!"
And I haven't.

I've done.
I've fought the pressure
The strain of it all
The tears
The ache of death
The smoke
Drink
The damned sun
      Forcing me to rise
            Face my new day

Over
&
Over
&
Over again.

We've given all we have
Every miniscule ounce
And still it beckons,
Unsatisfied.

I washed my hands
Before hugging my daughter
Hoping…
God damned praying
That it'll
Make
Some kind of difference.

Marriage

We have a long road
Ahead
Of us, my
Dear.

The songs play in
Our ears, feeding
Driving our continuance.
But it doesn't matter
Never did.

To be a 'We'
There has to be
More then
One
& I am one
With myself, my
Dear.

I gave up on
Life
To damned
Early.

& now there is regret
& sorrow, such sorrow
& love, I need
A release.

Depression

Depression
Is the
Key to it all,
The rights
To
Passage.

Depression
And it
Makes
Sense,
All
Of it
Makes
Sense.

The tears
The alcoholism
The futility
Of it
All
The depression
And reality is unblemished,
Clear.

I will sleep, now.
I will sleep
& I will dream.

Father Guardian

He stood in the darkness
Looking down at
His sleeping wife
& daughter.

And it was good,
Passionate in the sense
Of fatherhood,
Being a great husband.
The desire of family.

He stood there in the darkness
Dreaming of their tomorrows,
Contemplating
Their portrayal in his life.

The night a comfort
The murk vast
& mysterious.
Possibilities
Being endless.

He kissed the foreheads
Of his family
And turned
In…
Not sleepy
But tired.

At The Funeral & Nonina

I was standing beside my cousins
Our parents in front of us
As they carried Nonina
In her casket
Into the church
That morning.

It had been a long three
Days and the wake had
Taken its measure
On every soul of our
Family.

As they carried her
I looked around at those
Around me & I felt
Alien   I felt somehow removed
From them.

The lady in that casket
Had held my hand
As a child had loved me
When I wanted suicide
Had held my daughter
In her arms
The way
She had held me
After my birth.

The lady in that casket
I loved more then any,
More then myself…
And now she was gone.
Just like that.

I would call her each morning
Tell her how much
I loved her
And as I stood there
Behind my father
I thought
Who shall I call now?

Going to the burial site
I tried to sleep
In that long black limousine
But I couldn't
And when the tears
Wouldn't stop
I wanted
That bottle more
Then
I ever did in
All my
Life.

Don't Worry

He told me
"Don't worry, brother."
And I wanted to believe
Him
Tell him sure
I'll get over it
No problem
Trust me…I got it!
But I said nothing.

After we drank
Straight into the early morning
Hours of the following day
The night being as short
As it is

We parted ways
And
Though I felt
Somewhat better
I still didn't
Believe
Him.

Pablo Neruda

A good friend
Said to me this morning:
"You're the next Pablo Neruda."
And I smiled.

For him to compare me
To such a master…
For such a thing to be
Possible…
I felt that, maybe,
I had accomplished something.

I haven't had the time
To delve into Neruda's work
But I know of the
Legend.

One of the greatest poets
To have ever lived.

So I enjoyed the thought
Of such a comparison
For hours
And when I finally
Left work,
Got home in one piece,
Checked my mail,
And found two rejections

I thought…
'I guess the publishers
don't feel the same.'
And smiled,
Smiled like I had grown
In understanding.

To the people
I write like Neruda.
To the publishers
I'm a Bukowski wannabe.

DAMN!
I've accomplished
Exactly
What I wanted.

Comparison!

Toni, My Poetess

Toni got to work today
And said:
"I was writing until 2 o'clock
in the morning."
And I said:
"Congratulations!"

I feel she knows now
What it means
To
Be
A poet.

She has progressed
& become something
I didn't expect.
Pride & inspiration
Have
Taken over her true
Persona
And now
I see so much damned
Potential in her.

I read her work
Daily…
I love reading her work.

She has a flare
For Christ & his
Father.
So have I.

And with the grace of her beliefs
She will become great
In the Christian community
And I…
I will look on
With pride.

Enough Ammo

I'm reloaded!

And thus the road is paved
Short for many
Long for many
Longer still
For many more.

The struggle is never
Ending
Twisting & changing
Choice & destiny
Are left to be made in fear.

I'm reloaded!

A 9mm & a .22 caliber
Combined with a madman
& enough ammo to kill a small village
33 bodies.
The road is paved.
Virginia will never be the same
Again.

I'm reloaded!

3 bodies came 1st
Then a 15 minute stroll across campus

Then 30 more bodies.
The struggle is never
Ending.

One begins to think
Where was campus security?
One begins to feel
Nauseated at the fact
Of the killer taking
His stroll
Before concluding
The lives of 30 people,
Students
Children
Lovers
Brothers & sisters.

33 families demolished
Countless others left without
Their loved ones.
The numbers don't add up.

1 mans choice has
Confirmed the destiny
Of so many
Innocent people.

Several survivors
Explained how they barricaded
Their rooms to keep

The killer out.
I hope they'll explain
How disappointed they were
Towards the lack of response time
The so-called
Authority figures…
Protectors…
What ever the hell they
Call themselves;
Police…

And I hope these figures
Look back at the paved road
And say to themselves "Why?"
And feel their lack of response
And feel the 33 dead adolescents
And know in fear,
Now,
What sorrow is.

Kindness

There is kindness in the world
It's there.
Difficult at times to
Comprehend
But nonetheless it's
There.

Simply traveling public
Transportation
You can see it.
The giving of a seat
To another more in
Need.

Helping a blind man across the
Street. A complete
Stranger.

Sex with a cancer ridden woman.

There is kindness in this
World.
I can see it.

Isis & Her Bicycle

I watched you today,
Isis.
Riding your bike for the
First time
And God-damned
Me for a moment
But I swear
I cried
As you peddled.

In such a quick motion
You took a small
Lead
On me
And as I followed you,
Watching you,
Peddle
Following
I thought this is how
It should always
Be.

Shit Smeared

After reading my poetry
I notice
Several of my co-workers
Refrain
Shit smeared refrain
From speaking to me.
As if my face were
Horror
And my words
Were disease.

Before,
When ignorance of my persona
Rang home
There was acceptance.
Now, a few pages
Into *'Omega'* and
I'm an embarrassment.

Fuck it!
Fuck them!

I can't write it
Enough.

Fuck them.
Fuck them.
Fuck them. Fuck them. Fuck them.

Aaaaggggrrrhhh!
But then:
The written word isn't for
Every one.

Sense

For Savage

Only thing that makes sense to
Me
Is my poison.

Back At It Again

Back at it again
Devils are still tinglin'
Bangin' on the linin' of my
Skull.

Back at it again
Lookin' for a story
I ain't yet told
For a line I ain't yet wrote.

I hear a sentence
Streaming in flashing purity
Ragin' in my head
Tellin' me in quick succession
Death is the road to awe.

$2 + 2 = 4$
two plus two equals four.

And maybe Dostoevsky
The great gambling novelist,
Creator of tomes,
Was right.

The shortest path
From one point to the next
Is a straight line.

Back at it again
Damn angels leavin' me
To my sin.

I think I am the poet
Therefore I am
The poem therefore
I am the poem
The poem.

Yeah, my love.
That's right! I need convincing
Like crap needs an asshole.

Let's go at it
You and me.
Let's get back at it
Again.

Not Enough

I love you, Isis
But not enough to want
To continue my life.

I love you, Isis
Though I've drank my liver away
Though my lungs are black with nicotine.

I love you.

I hold your feet in my hands
Hover over you
Look into your eyes
And I love you.

But not enough to want
To continue my life.

The rejections have worn me thin
And the futility of it all has wrung home.
My little love
Through it all I still love you.

And, yes, I think now
When the day comes for your turn
At rejecting me
I will stand there hands in my pocket

And tell you
I always & shall always love you.

That it only mattered
That my love for you
Has always & always
Been the only reason
I ever made it as far
As I have.

A Break In The Routine

This morning, sun shining, birds chirping
Not a cloud in the sky
Or sadness in any eye I met...
Something fantastic happened
And as great as it was
I can't shake my feelings
Of gratitude and astonishment.

Going to work
I stepped in a great big pile of
Dog shit.
Smiling
I thought finally the routine
Had changed. I thought
Of a cycles end & beginning.

Stepping in that shit
It covered my shoe
Smeared up onto my pants
And socks and
I thought
Finally... difference.

Tomorrow
On my way to work
I'm going to find the biggest
Meanest looking pile of shit

And put both my feet
Into it…
I'm going to give it
All
I
Got.

The Barbarian At The Theater

At the theater
During the entirety of the
Film, this obnoxious creature,
A broken remnant of courtesy
Talked through every scene.

During every classic horror
Moment this asshole
Had something to say.

I wanted to tear his fucking heart
Out of his god-damned chest.

But Vero quickly calmed me
With:
"Please, Carlos! Your daughter…
It's Mothers Day."
So I sat in silence and for me
That movie was ruined.

A Trip Into Jersey

Got out of the city yesterday
The madness of it all
And took a trip over to Jersey.

We went into this supper shopping
                             Center.
For a while, upon entering, there
Was a dominant feeling
Of awe
At how much merchandise was stocked
In this super store
At the calm resonating
Through my fellow shoppers
Faces.

An immediate feeling of
Alienation
Filled into my lungs
My loins
Shriveled and hid.
My heart fluttered
& I couldn't be in such
A placid environment.

The Damned city is in my DNA.

I took a long pull on my cigarette
Once my ordeal was at

An end &
Looked up into the sky
Feeling as if even the sky
Itself
Were some new experience.

On our way back to the city
I tried to sleep
Tried to relax.
If I ever bring myself
To have enough courage
To return
To Jersey

I'll kiss my wife
Good-bye
Just in case…
Just
In
Case
I don't make it back.

Machine Throat

They have these men, tired, grungy looking
On TV hold machines to their necks
And complain of cigarettes
And nicotine
And how never again
They'll be able to talk
With their natural God-given voices.

They try to rape sympathy
Awareness & crap of the sort
Out of everyone
Dead on their couches
Listening to the broadcast.

During this one particular
Commercial
I had just finished taking a
Great big shit
While smoking my nicotine
And I thought
I wonder how many times
This zombie fuck robot voiced
Cock sucker
Smoked a cigarette while shitting?

Well, after wiping my ass
With the remains of some dead tree
Seeing that man invading the

Privacy of my home
I went out onto the porch
Lit up another cigarette
And using the best robot voice
I was capable of
Said:

"My name is Carlos & I smoke
cigarettes and piss & shit blood
and yes… I have a strange lump in my head
just above the hair line."

And I finished my smoke
Thinking all the while
Of my next session.

Simplistic Nature

Nature is in bloom
Birds and squirrels
Pack the trees
Making the best
Of their tiny lives.

And their tiny lives
Meaning so much
to me.
Drunk, sober, it doesn't
Matter how I view them
As long as they remain.

Just their being,
Their simplicity,
Puts my soul
At ease.

Man Vs. Child

A puff…
The smoke bathes over my face,
The need quenched,
Desire silenced
For a moment.

A chance glance
As I watch the smoke ascend
And my heart breaks.

Some man,
Some giant of a man,
Pushes his child
Against his car
Back hands the boy
In the face
And looks up to find me
Staring
Standing
Ready to defend a child
I've never met.

He quickly gets into his car
The crying child
Follows.
I take a long hard drag
Upset at such abuse
And pray to God for the first time

In a very long time
For that man to die
Some gruesome death.

I flicked my cigarette into
The wind
And climbed the stairs
Back into my apartment.

A Family Veneer

A small family of four
Travel to work together
Each morning.

The husband, a young man
The wife, a young woman
And their two sons
All together
And I think this
Is how a family
Should look.

They hold hands
Smile
Laugh
And you get the feeling
They're above reality.

After a week or so
Of seeing this constant
Happiness
It starts to eat away at
Your stomach.

Sometimes beauty will
Do that to you.

All You Can Try

The trees are a luscious
Life green with burnt bark
Reflecting brick tombs of man.
They give to us & we take from them
Like fat bastards at a buffet

Like an alcoholic with the rent
In his pocket stuck in a liquor
Store with an empty grocery basket.

The Chinaman collects the cans
The Blackman, too.
A good night can clear you
With $50 tax-free in the pocket.

I'd rather wipe my ass
With the trees
And drink what's in the cans
With my rent money.

The Hindu's run the liquor store,
The Arab runs the grocery,
They both know me well.

The Dominicana owns the bodega
& sells all the smoke.
She Id's me always
Though I pass her in the street

Puffing great plumes of nicotine
Into her pretty face.

I'm trying to kill her with 2nd hand.

The Yellow man looks at me with horror.

The Black man calls me brother.

The Brown man… he's uncertain…
As uncertain as myself.

Blue streaks above my head
And spots before my eyes
The trees look lovely
The alcoholics
Smokers
& can collectors
All of them… so lovely.

Give Your Ass To Everything

Suppose for one moment
You let go of it all
Turned your back to the world
Pulled your pants down
& gave your ass to everything
You left behind.

Really, it can't be all that bad
To give your self such relish,
To embrace such uncertainty.

When you're at your last ounce of lager
The butt of your cigarette
Brown filth & finished.
Think about it…
Why run anymore?

Pull out your cock or bare your cunt!

Chances are you'll be imprisoned
For indecent exposure as well
As a host of murder & rape charges.
But what the hell
They'll never be able to say you
Didn't give life
All you had.

Old Chick With Style

There's this elderly lady
Elegant & beautiful as little as
Thirty years ago.

She puffs away at cigars
& I'm like that's a woman
With class and all that.
I mean I'd love
To sit with her one morning
And talk.

Ask her about the men she
Used to know, used to fuck, etcetera.
Where's she been?
How's it been getting to
The right now?

Aaaagggrrhhh! Circumstances
Wouldn't allow such a verbal
Exchange.

If she doesn't think I'm
Trying to rob her
She'd probably call me a pervert
And I'd be forced to
Praise her ability
To observe a situation…
Her ability to see the truth of it all.

A Taste & Then: Return

The frigid New York air
Brings life to my tarred lungs.
Goose flesh.
Desire to remain home
In peace.

I suck in oxygen like a God
Consuming a full course meal,
Like an addict with a kilo
Lying on his lap and all the
Time in the world.

When leaving my home
To embrace the city
And all its maniacs
Prostitutes
Reverends
& cab drivers,
Before lighting my cigarette

I breathe in some life.
Not too much…
Just enough to keep me going.

The knot in my stomach
Fades off for a moment
And through the honking
Of highways traffic

The chirping of sparrows
In half dead trees.
My heart thunders on
Pounding rhythms of passion
Into my bloodstream.

For that simple moment
That first intoxicating second
Of perfect purity
I feel free.

Then I lift my cigarette
To my mouth
And face the routine.

One Month Clean

These hardships
They come at you like monuments
Of burden prepared, hungry,
For your life.

I gave myself a one month
Poetry break and here I am
Scribbling, writing, trying
To make sense.

When you run away from something
Whatever it may be
Eventually, it'll catch up to you
Rip your heart out, chew it,
Spit it back at you
And call it a day's work.

You'll stand there
Head in hands
Tears all spent
Wondering what in the hell
Happened.

Fist Fight & Death Stayed Home

Saw something so spectacular
A fist fight. Beautiful as it was
In this day and age…
To see a fist fight
Is a rarity.

Two woman, mere girls,
Surrounded by teenagers of their sort
Went blow for blow
One on one.
It lasted maybe 15 seconds
But the purity it created
Was remarkable.

It ended with their backs
Turned to one another
As they both walked away
In opposite directions.

Standing, I felt grateful.
The world was still a bit
Civilized… Those two girls
Could have used guns on one another
And instead of fist play
Death could've rung home.

Can't Write
What You Don't Know

Brad came to me with words
Of disappointment & honesty.
He spoke of a relative
A poet, young, sheltered,
Whose poems are built of crime,
Horrors & uncertainty.

"His poems are only about violence.
Only things on television. Things from
The music videos. I want him to read your
Work. I want him to know truth
& reality."

Quietly, looking down, clarity of thought
Fleeing from my possession.
Regret invaded my eyes,
Sorrow my ears.
Brad read my work and saw pain
And now… now I am a model,
A mascot to learn from.

I told Brad I hope his relative
Enjoys my work
And as I walked off
I thought
'Because I hated living it.'

Self-Destructive

Hungover
Rotten inside, alcohol singed
My eyes bloodshot
Hands shaking
Hair falling out
And by choice
I have elected this.
The label on the can of lager
Shall be my death certificate.

I have fallen
I cannot fall because
I have already fallen.

The lowest of the low
Alcoholic poet filled with confusion
And sorrow
And rejection
I am finally tired.

I don't want drink anymore.

So much to do, to be, to see.
Got to get back up, fight,
Say good-bye to the bottle

My daughter…
She told me she loves me.

Three years old and she loves me.
I feel this love might be enough
To save me
From myself.

I pray that it is enough.

Music: Just Right

Here, on my porch,
Stars above and behind my awning,
Chester Bennington
Makes sense. His voice,
His words… Rafi said
Chester's lyrics are too sad.
Joey said the lyrics are too weak.
For me: they're just right.

Flames of my cigarette ascend
With the chorus of
"The little things give you away."
And it all makes sense
The bottle
Buk
Dost
Palahniuk
They all make sense.

When the songs over
My cigarette finished
I feel used
Carried to a point of enlightenment
And then let loose
Amongst
The broken maniacs
Wondering the night streets.

Tattooed

I paid for a man to stab ink
Into my skin with a needle
Attached to a small motor.

Buzzing in my ears
Sweat streamed off my forehead
From a combination of a 100 watt lamp
And fear of pain.

Tattooed.
One hour and the artist had finished.
My arm holds a piece of his art,
His livelihood.

"You took the pain well." He said.
Continuing. "What were you thinking about?"

Looking at the swelling of my arm
The blood filled paper towels in
His waste basket…
I answered: "Nothing."
And I didn't lie.

The terrible pain
Sharp as it was
Held onto me in such a loving embrace
I thought nothing
But felt apart of everything.

Savage was up next.
A portrait of the devil on his arm.

The buzzing needle.

He flinched and said: "I remember!"
"Fuck! It hurts." Looking at me
Knowing that I had faced his burden
Minutes before he did.

The artist smiled.
"Take it easy, Savage."

Later, while he and I returned home
He asked what it was I had
Thought of while getting *inked-up*
& I answered:
"Nothing."
And
I
Didn't lie.

"You took the pain, Carlos." He exclaimed.
And I said:
"No! I let the pain take me.
So when we doing this again."

And he said not
For a long
Time.

Persecutor

A lady tripped
And
Almost fell before catching
Herself.

Just happening to pass by
I asked: "You alright, Mrs.?"
And she said yes
Disappearing into the city streets.

Vero, with me at the time, immediately
Moved away from me.
"You ignore me but show so much
concern for total strangers!"

I kept quiet.
The thirst was upon me like
Teeth in my mouth.

We went into the grocery store.
"What are you buying?" She asked.
"Beer."

"Alcoholic!" She spits.

Walking home I thought, can in hand,
When would someone stop me
And ask if I'm alright?

Maybe then
With my luck
Life
Wouldn't be so un-
Fucking-
Bearable.

I May Be Drunk

She came into the bedroom
As I gulped at my lager
And stood there, fuming
Eyes red with murder
Hands tense with violence.

"All you do is drink!"

"Oh, shit!" I say.

"Why don't you just kill yourself?" She asks.

I see my daughter playing at the foot
Of my bed
As her mother questions me.

"I'm trying."
"Well," she starts. "You're not doing it fast enough."
And smiling I say:
"Yeah… you could say that again."

Leaving me to my death, can still in hand,
I smiled as Isis played with
Her toys. She stopped, looked
At me and asked:
"Why're you so sad, Daddy?"

Changing the subject I said:

"Tomorrow we should go to Toys R us."

"Yeah, Daddy!" And she was so happy
And as for Vero & wanting my
Death…
I'll have to do it the day after
Tomorrow.

Because Whatever The Fuck

I don't look up to you
Because
You're beside me

I don't hate you
Because
You hate me

I don't pity you
Because
You pity me

I don't question you
Because
You question me

I don't look up to you
Because
You're behind me

I don't hassle you
Because
You hassle me

I don't fight you
Because
You fight me

I don't wish your death
Because
You wish mine

I don't look up to you
Because
My dreams are
Co-dependent
Upon your adversity

So…
Don't you ever stop
Your being against
Everything I am
Because
There won't be an 'US'
Anymore.

Vero & The Discovery

Such sadness has come over
My Vero.
Such sadness she's never known.
Death has a way with
Reality.
No other aspect
Can ever shed such clarity.

Vero lost a coworker
In some tragic accident.
Now she sits in remembrance
In tears
Trying to hold onto every
Moment
Every smile
Every word the two shared.

I've tried to find words
To give her some comfort
But I know
Only time
Can heal the sickness of loss.
So I limit my words while trying to
Convince her
The pain will pass.

But I know it won't.

I tell her to dwell
On good memories
If dwelling is her objective.

& yes, I envy her sadness
I envy it and her
Because she faces it
Alone.
I would have given into
The bottle without a moment's hesitation.

She is so strong,
So precious.
There aren't words I may
Say to comfort her
But I have life.
So when she feels the burden
The loss creeping up
I will remain beside her

Let her feel my presence.
Let her know we stand together,
That I grieve with her.

Pitiful Men

This world
Is
Built
By pitiful
Men.

Yes,
I wish
For the world
Constructed
Solely
By the barbarian.

At least
The barbarian
Has clear
Intentions.

These politicians
With their
Insane
Sophistication
Are going to
Murder
The world
With their
Innuendos.

My Little Brother

My little brother
Lost in your deceit & lies
I look upon you
Now
In a disappointment
That could carve
Rage into
A mans eyes.

My little brother
I know your path
For I have lived it
And it is built
Of
Stupidity.

Branded

The nine rings of Dante's Hell
Are branded into my soul.
The branding iron
Heated with the Devils blood
Brought to a point of uselessness…
The metal white hot.

Yes, I once followed Christ
And still I feel his love
But the road I travel…
It has lead me astray
Blackening my soul
With unforgivable acts
Of madness.

And life…
I thirst for its
Conclusion.

The Sand In-Between My Toes

The sand in-between my toes
Ocean air caressing my scalp
Oh, the terrible disproportioned
Bodies
Bathing in the sun
Have eyes of familiarity.

We look upon each other
Like mirrors filled with lies
Mirrors built not of glass
But soul and cigarette smoke.
A shard of seashell
Slicing into the body
With ease
And hope
And it's how it's always
Been,
Useless.

They walk across the sea & sand
On the borders of here & there
Waiting for purpose to rise up
Out of either direction,
But as always
Find nothing.

I walk beside them
Taking my time with it
Enjoying my birth
Into nothing…
Being nothing.

My daughter
Splashing the waves
Smiling and playing
Within the currents
I look on her
Smile & keep going.

She has her own path
As mine is to follow
The horde
And drown
In limbo
A creature of failure.

Faces

Old faces
Bring back memories
Of a past
That once was
But is no more.

Time is at loss
When old faces meet
And nothing else
Nothing else
Matters…
Not moments of pain
Or pleasure…
Moments of lost love
Or newly given life.

All that matters
Are the face we now hold
And what it meant to us
Then…
What it could have meant
To us… then.

A sip on my can
A tug on my cigarette
And it all makes sense.

"Fuck It!"

A guzzle on the life giving
Sustenance and I am free
Of the haggard tortures of
The moment
The mundane moment
Crisp

Clean shaven shit
That's supposed to mean something
Anything more then what it is.

I lift the can to my lips
The bud to my lips
And I make sense
Of my sense of being.

The publishers…
They say it's easy to write:
"Fuck it!"
But I know it's not.
To have such strength –
"Fuck it!"
"Fuck it!" –
One must suffer the madness
Of a broken life
A life like that of an abused
Child

Born of hemp
And loved by drink.

A father at constant odds
With his children.
A father with hatred – rage
In his heart.
"WHORE!" He called his daughter.
"FAGGOT!" He called his son.

I lift the can to my lips
The bud to my lips
And I make sense
Of my sense of being.

I will not falter
Will not consider
How lost
I am.

Tomorrow…
Tomorrow's another day.
"Fuck it!"

Alex Has Everything Under Control

Alex
He tells me he's alright
That things for him
Are great
Are really under his control.

And like I'm supposed to be
An asshole
A dumb asshole
Convinced of his lies
I "Yes!" him
I "Yes!" him as if dreams
Were on sale
& souls were a dime
A dozen.

He'll learn of life
Through experience
And I'll look on
A cousin
With understanding.

Heroes

Hitler, Amin, Castro,
Columbus, Hussein, Milosevic

Berkowitz, Dahmer, Gacy,
Gein, Kurten, Gotti

Some people in this world
Consider these men
Heroes.
They look upon them with love
Respect, cherish the actions
& pleasures they indulged.

Trujillo
Goebbels
Zedong
Bush (both of them)

I want no more heroes
Of any sort.

Give me the wino
The heroine addict.
Give me the nicotine fiend
And the lager bum on a city bench.

Genghis Khan
Napoleon
The entire CIA.

I want no more heroes
Of any sort.

No promises of unity…
A better world
Or struggle before peace.

Drug everyone and put us in cells
Filled with

Bibles
Korans
Torahs & etcetera.

Give us Dostoevsky
Clavell, a little Wilde
Some Lorca & Neruda
A dash of Bukowski.

& time… it doesn't matter.

I want no more heroes
Of any sort.

I'm so tired of putting on
My television & hearing & seeing
Death, sex, Munchausen Biproxy.

I want to set across the horizon
Drunk & high…
Broken & forgotten.

Problem + Bullets = Intelligence

It's the mundane nonsense
That breaks a person's stamina
Rips to shreds any hope they may
Have had at making it
Through their day.

Usually it's other people
Stirring such madness
Dishing it out like free crap.

These people fertilize
The world with their
Stupidity
& look on proud of their
Accomplishments.

You stand there
Fed up with it all
Scream out:
"Fuck EVERYTHING!"
And then
With a smile born of victory
They acknowledge
Your weakness
With disciplinary actions.

Straight Jackets
Wrist and ankle shackles

A pad or concrete cell
No communication with the outside
World from fear of your contaminating
The populace.

My father used to tell me
He had a bullet for all of them.

Then: I used to mock him.

Now: I envy his intelligence.

School, Again

Across
The boundaries of everyday life
Over the can of beer
The smoked cigarette
28 years of age
I have begun my return
To school.

I wonder at how it will be
To sit in a classroom
And learn
Again.

I pray to learn something
Life hasn't already
Punished me with…
Something pure & innocent
Something I can use
To better support
My drinking

And mostly my daughter.

Manic Depressive

I've discovered
I'm manic depressive.
It feels great to finally
Know what's been killing
Me
All these years.

There were several symptoms
And I have all of them.
Some more than others
But nonetheless
All of them.

I've scheduled an appointment
With a psychiatrist
Though I feel it won't
Help
My situation.

Unless
Of course
The doc prescribes me some
Really awesome drugs
To kill my mind.

Insomniac
Anxious
Mood swinger

Headache ridden
Stomach ache
Suicidal
Self destructive
Alcoholic
Weight fluctuating
Useless emptiness
Futile
Smoker.

Yup!
Hopefully the doc will give me
Some really awesome drug
That'll give me some peace…
Some hope.

Tai Chi Bullshit

Tai chi in the park
With trees and squirrels
Birds and bugs
Meditation through concentration
Concentration through meditation
These practitioners fight
To achieve
An enlightenment unparalleled
A clean righteous understanding
Of their selves
& their world
However mundane
However banal it may be.

They breathe
Engulf themselves in movement
Stretch themselves thin
Across the fertile
Ground.

Ridiculous!

You can achieve the same purpose
With so much ease
120 ounces or better known as
3 forties
And **BANG!**
The universe will hold

Not a single secret
From
You.

Ghost With Drink & Smoke

I look up to the stars
As billions have done,
As trillions will do.

Humanity will go on long
After I have found
My peace
With the calm of death.

If I can look on
I will   not that I would
Want to   but
Rather then participate
In the chaos of it all
I'd prefer to watch.

Like watching the stars
Hitching a ride from
An unknown stranger
Heading nowhere
Special.

Yes, to drink and smoke
& look on at what
I never felt
Apart of
Would
Give me such satisfaction.

As tonight
Just like all
Nights
Before & after.

The stars look
So tempting.

Illiterate Retard

He was a giant of a man
7' with a brain
That didn't work so well
So right
Our society viewed him
As mildly
Retarded.
He couldn't read
Couldn't write his name
Worked a minimum wage job
Tried as hard as he could
To appear normal.

Whenever not at work
He voluntarily
Took care of his infant nephew
Carrying him wherever
His feet could carry him
The tiny child
Appeared so at ease
In the giant arms of his
Uncle.

As I watched the two
In the Laundromat one night
I felt their love
For one another
The child never ridiculed him

Never called him illiterate
Never felt for a second
His uncle was anything less
Then a man he himself
Wanted to grow up to be.

And it was beautiful
Feeling their love.

And as for the giant
For as long as life was his
He was sure of one important
Fact…
He'd use his life
To protect his nephew
Sacrifice it willingly
Without ever questioning
Without any falter.

Our society views this man
As an illiterate retard.
I view him as a perfect example
Of priceless phenomena.

Started On The Seroquel

The Docs started me
On something called Seroquel
After their diagnosis.
It's the same shit
They treat schizophrenics
With.

I guess the schizo
& manic are so alike
Their cure is the…
Has no…
Can be considered
The same.

Doc said I'd have to give up
My lager when taking
Seroquel   also said I should
Stop smoking.

"Your heart may not be able
to take the strain."

Isis sat with me
During the diagnosis
& when the doctor
asked when was the last time
I was happy
I said: "When she was born."

"And before that?"
"Don't think I ever was."
"Suicide?"
"I dream about it. I don't like
to sleep."

The diagnosis went on
As Isis sat quietly
Beside me.
She never moved
Listening.

And though I felt like
Killing the doctor for
"Knowing how I felt"
She kept me at bay, smiling,
Each time I looked at her.

"Well, I'm going to give you
the prescription. What do you
think
about that, Carlos?"

And looking at Isis
I answered:
"Thank you."
And my daughter smiled
Happy
&
I was happy, too.

Song Of Sparrows

3 days have passed since I began
My plunge into a world of numbing
Hell born of plastic bottles
With my name pasted to them like
A death notice.

Vero tells me with ever-loving words
How my eyes look drunk
And my speech is slurred.
She holds my hand showing
Affection and concern.

The moon sways in and out
I cannot focus my emotions
Feel worn but death is no longer
An option. Seroquel has me
Where I choose to be…
Where the song of sparrows
Prolong space & time.

Joey tells me with ever-envious words
How I don't need the mind crap
All I need is a moment of freedom
But, my brother, this state of
Zombified-spirit, this is my
Destiny. I do not want death
Suicide or any cide.

The blood in me is black, tainted,
Distorted with sloth & shadows
The dreams of my nights
Are flashes of brilliance
Slit throats and blow torched
Faces. No,
My wife,
My brother, though I am now
A drugged man, a lover of alcohol
And nicotine.

The sky…

Looking up to it
I know
Something
Is terribly wrong.
But whatever the hell it is
My new found barbiturate
Has it at bay.

Toni

Toni, my friend
Standing there so concerned
For my well being
So ready to share a word
Of faith with me.
You alone encompass one
Stark truth:
No other can see my soul.

But then there's you
So ready to listen
Wanting me to listen
In some strange way sharing
One another.
My dear friend
I am life without life
A smile without happiness
A frown without sadness
A death without death.

When you wake each morning
There's a fire burning within
Your chest.
A massive pyre of flame & hope
Driving you on
Forcing you to fight

To give every breath you take
One hundred percent of everything
You are.

I lack even the courage
To wake each day.

My life feels like a film
That's just ended, the credits
Are rolling and as the last
Name scrolls by, my name,
No one remains
To read it
To read it and know, yes,
Know I was there…
I did something.

Toni, my dear friend
You should have given up
On me long ago.
You should have left me
On the shoreline
Naked and scorched
I do not deserve you
But, I cherish you
Damn,
How I cherish you.

Immaculate Drink

It's been so long
Since I last enjoyed
The comforts of strong
Immaculate drink.
My flesh feels burdened
By a thirst nothing else
Seems to satisfy
And , yes, if God permits it
I will soon return
To my lager.

Vero will look at me with eyes
& soul embraced by disappointment
And I will smile
Smile with the soundless speech
Of "It is my choice".

She's already consumed with doubt
Angry beyond the point of
Forgiveness
And I do not blame her.
She has every right
To despise me.
My failure
Is her failure.

My mind feels tortured
As my body no longer

Remembers redemption.
I'm an alcoholic
I'm a veneer of humanity
Wasted & worthless

And though I recognize this
I wait.
$1.99 and I wait
For my salvation.

Lust Is Such A Fucked-Up Sin

Torn between a realm of
Drugged & distorted truths
I entered the bus
With my eyes so happily glued
To the floor.
It was pure burden making my
Way to an empty seat in the back
Up against the engine.

So conscious of my footing
I managed to melt into the chair
Take a deep breath
& look at the faces
Surrounding me.

3 woman sat in front of me
When I noticed the one
Dressed to kill
I fought not to look
At the cleavage being pushed
Into my line of sight

& better yet
the tremendous smile
accompanied with it.

I quickly adjusted my glasses
With my left hand

Praying to break the tide
With her seeing
The wedding band on my
Ring finger.

But things got worst
And as the nipple came
Into view I could do
Nothing but pretend to sleep.

Damn that low dosage!

If my dosage had been massive
Drool pouring from my mouth
Maybe she wouldn't have
Flaunted her body…
Wouldn't have had
Given her self to my eyes.

When it was time to leave
The bus stopping at my stop
I stood
Looked down
Counted my steps & thinking
Of Vero
I exited
Without ever looking back.

Lust is such a fucked-up sin!
It makes one wish he were
Blind, deaf & dumb.

Don't Confuse Sympathy

Never been much for actual sympathy
Stuff like that clouds the
Judgment
And before you know it
The receivers of your acknowledgements
Will start thinking
You give a damn
That you actually wholeheartedly
Care.

No, I've never found sympathy
To be an honest – to – God
Admirable
Quality.

15 Minutes

For a living I punch a card
So the organization paying me will know
I was actually present for
The allotted time of
My obligation.

Most of us punch cards
That time clock controls
So many of our destinies
And it's as if our existence
Can know no other way.

M., my boss, head honcho
King Kahuna, checks my
Record and tells me one
Day during the pay period
I came 4 minutes late
Smiling   I apologized
For my inexcusable neglect

And thought
"I don't give a rat's ass!"
She continued:
"A minute late and we're allowed
to take fifteen minutes off your pay."

And then I thought:
"Fuck if I care! After

everything I've done
for the people here!"

The favors…
The politics…
And you think I care for
15 minutes…
I never cared for money.

If M. wasn't such a great person
I'd have told her
I take drugs so I won't kill
Myself.
What in this world would make you
Think I care for 15 minutes?
But instead I said:

"It won't happen, again."
And it was left
At that.

Birth Of A Murderer

He stalked
Across the room
Back & forth
The medication began
Its phase
Slowly
& the drowsiness
Had started
Its course
Devouring his consciousness
And his ability
To tell right
From wrong.

Aunt Margie, I Miss You

We stood out there together
Smoking our cigarettes,
Laughing & talking.

"If you ever need anything, Carlos."
"I know."
"I'll always be here for you."
"I know."

And she looked so beautiful
With the sunlight
The wind
Playing upon her entire person.

Her body was swollen with water
Retention & her arms black & blue
From the constant blood
Transfusions & withdrawals.

"You sure it's alright to smoke
out here?" I asked.
"The nurses are nice in this hospital?"
"Are they?"
"I can't wait for you to get out of here."

She took a long drag on her cigarette
While holding onto the balcony rail.

"As soon as I get out of here
we're all going to Great Adventures."
I remained silent
Relishing our moment together.
The sound of sirens wailing
In the distance
The song of sparrows filling
The halls of heaven.

"How's your wife?" she asked.
"Good." I answered, exhaling 2nd hand.
"And your daughter?"
"I love her so much."
"I can't believe you named her after me."

When our cigarettes were finished
As we walked back to her room
Weak from cancer, dieing,
She held my arm.

I stayed with her until she fell
Asleep.
I kissed her forehead and
I loved her like stars love
The night sky.

I think of her now
Up there in the heavens.
She's been gone two years,
Two long & painful years.

A Call Of Unity

Some African Tribal music
Some fantastic African Tribal music
Pounding rhythm into the soul
Heartbeat
Heartbeat
Pounding into the chest
Making the world seem impossible
But so very attainable.

The children listen
Snapping their fingers
Becoming apart of the beat
Trying, with the music,
To make sense of their lives
With sound.

The five woman of the band
Bring movement to the floor
And what was once dull
Is now lively. Dreams
Through their hands
Are dished out for the multitudes.
For their power of rhyme
Extends to even those
Who cannot feel the magnificence
Of sound.

Heartbeat
Heartbeat
The beat rips into the chest
Gives meaning
Strips the boundaries of reality.

I have had my chance here
Amongst the youth and the band.
But I, stubborn,
Deny my being
Deny their calling for unity
Through the drum.

I abandon them.
I retreat into the shadows
Of my truth and touch base
With what matters most to me.

Plug up my ears
& ignore my heart.

I take a long powerful
Gracious drag on my
Cigarette.

The solitude & now
The drums in the distance
Far from my reach
I have found my heartbeat…
Silence.

A Toast Of Pride

You tell yourself there's meaning
That there has to be purpose.
The lies become rich with
The stench of falsehood.

You've devoured the grace that
Was once your innocence.

Standing with the sins of
Your livelihood you understand
You are, you are
And it'll be until the day
You pass on.

So for you,
For me,
A toast   raising our glasses high:
"We've got no chance,
never did. We were born
into this screaming & naked.
So with outstanding strength
& determination we embrace
Our pride and shout into the
Heavens: FUCK IT!"

Preparation For School

It's an alienation,
Unfamiliar to the physicality
Of my life.
Comprehension of an action
I no longer understand.

Picture me almost thirty
Trying to go back to school
Trying to better myself
In society
When all I want to do
Is drink, smoke, &
Enjoy the comforts of solitude.

It's a strange attempt
On my part to have even
Considered
What I now seek.

School?
Trade school?

My wife tells me there's no harm
In trying,
No harm in bettering myself
But I think what if
I'm more then satisfied
With what I am?

What if
I've already come to terms
With the futility
Of it all?

Of course, I could voice this
But that would be futility
& disappointment dished out
To the one person who wouldn't
Accept my so-called failure…

Because in her eyes
Doing noting is failure.

So I move towards
What she considers correct
Though in my heart
I no longer expect
Anything from the life
I live.

Except my smoke
& my drink.

Too Poor For School

Plans get mutilated
If you don't have the money
To follow through.

I guess I really wanted
To go back to school.
But after hearing it'll
Cost me $45,000
I'm finished with it.

Where's my beer?

The Violence Of Gods

Our bodies like machines
Work in a perfect motion
Completely unison
Moist, o, how we were oiled
With passion.

Ejaculation.

We move.
We move.
And the world outside.

Doesn't mean a damned
Thing   never did   never will
We make love. Fuck like
Dragons in heat   like sparrows
In flight. And this is ours.

No one can tarnish what we've done
What we have submitted our flesh
To.   Do you want it   yes   yes
O, yes!
I, finely oiled piece of machinery,
I am yours. Lightning in a dream.
You are my thunder.

Sweet love, O how we fucked
With the violence of gods.

The Poet Needs Pain

Buk was right
In his infinite reason.
The poet needs pain
The poet needs it like his typewriter
His Microsoft Word document
His blank page & pen or pencil or chalk
Or whatever-the-fuck.

Damn that old man dead
In his grave. Books polluting
My life   Chinaski all over
My train of thought.

He's the one writer
I've ever read
Who possessed a keen
Knowledge of me.
His beer is my beer
My cigarette his…
Our woman: ours…

And goddamned how I love
The solitude & distance.

Before the AA meetings
Before I knew of Buk
I woke to a pint of vodka
Every single useless day.

Now, years later,
When I wake with the thirst
I hear Buk in my head
Telling me to
"Go all the way!"

So I listen & long-hand
As many poems as I can
The damn things
Pour out of me like mucus
Diarrhea and what-not.

Old man, wherever you are
I know you have a beer in hand
One day I'll pull up a stool
And sit beside you.
After your drink we'll
Go out back or out front
And go a few rounds…
Really bust each other down.

Meanwhile, I have lots of work
To do, poems to write
Stories to tell
Sex to be had
Poison to be sought
Dreams to be lost.

Mismatched Slippers

The fatigue settles in
& the pen is heavy
& walking
Takes on a life of its own.

Headed out of the house
Sliding into a pair of slippers
I stumbled my way to the bus
A took a seat upon its arrival.

Within 3 bus stops
I was dead asleep
Dead asleep with my fellow
Passengers
Looking – staring at me.

I was too tired to care.

My stop came and I exited
About half-dead.
Somehow I discovered
My place of work
Changed my clothes
In a very very slow motion.

When chance brought to attention
A great misshapen horror.
My slippers were different

I had worn
Two different slippers
For one hour while
Traveling the domain
Of the most scrutinizing
Society time has ever known.

Whatever got into me
During the night
Left me borderline retarded.

I called Vero
And she, after laughing
Hysterically
Said:
"Take a taxi home, Stupid."

& as I walked to the
Taxi base   eyes
Burning into my botched
Toes
I began to hate society
And its tremendous
Expectations of its
Citizens.

Ejaculate On The Bees

The bees swirl around the weeds
Looking for a partner
To mate with. All flowers
Have insect partners.
Pollination & crap of the sort.

Bees & plants
Fuck
More then humans do.
The plants ejaculate
What they will onto the bee
And that dirty old bee
Flies over
To the next plant
Rubs some ejaculate on it
And
Kazam! Presto!
We have pollination.

Now, take an average male
He ejaculates all over his wife
Goes down stairs to the
Next woman
Ejaculates on her
And
Kazam! Presto!
We have pollination.

Boxing Gloves

Me & Ralf
Strap on the boxing gloves
And we go at it for dreams
Like mongers on crack.

Punch after punch
We think of Palahniuk's
'Fight Club'
Each blow
Sculpting our bodies
Building ourselves into perfection.

He is a Tyson-type
Where as I tend to lean towards
A Chavez-type.

It's so great
How each blow
Makes us
Under-
Stand
Brotherhood
That much
More.

The Alcoholic Of Awe

While at the bus stop
A squirrel ran up to me
And started to wipe its face
Clean with its miniature
Hands.
I said: "Good morning, Little Brother."
And the other people
Waiting with me,
A bald man
& a woman with holes spotting her jeans,
Looked at me in awe.

Madness Of The Masses

The summer heat brings out
The madness of the masses.
Woman stalk the city sidewalks
Half naked begging to be raped
Or mutilated.
I stand there witness to this
With half a mind…
Half a desire to become
That rapist
That mutilator.

They all use lust to benefit
Their separate situations,
To further their personal goals.

Then there are the men
Showing their physique
Six packs and tremendous
Biceps. No, I'm not as
Jealous of them as if,
Lets say,
I had their physique…
No envy here.
Just a desire to stand toe-to-toe
With them and really
Slug it out
Show'em what the skinny
Alcoholic can do.

Take a second
It may be overcoming
& breathe.
The women are just women.
The men just men.
All just broken dreams
Amongst broken dreams.

Yes, I'd like to kill'em all
And if it weren't for beer
I'd have long killed myself.

But we can't always have what we want.

Drugged Voyeur

Sweet lovers on a staircase
A long climb ahead of them.
Children with training wheels
On their bicycles
A long road beneath them…
Before them.
Young men on the diamond of a
Baseball field, practicing
Perfecting a craft of millionaires.

A kiss from the lovers…
The children pick up speed…
A young man catches a ball…

Their dreams…
I envy their dreams.

Kylie

For Lenny and her newborn

I saw the stars in your eyes
I saw my dreams in your smile
Kylie, you give me hope
When you're in my arms.

The curls of your hair,
The feel of your heart
Against mine.
Your warmth and smell…
O, how you smell like
Everything I could ever
Want.

It's so strange
Watching you grow.
Seems just like yesterday
I was so alone
So without you.

But, now, like the blossoming
Of a flower
Like the song of a sparrow
You are my life.

I wash your feet
Fighting for your dreams
Prepared to give myself

Body& soul
For your happiness.
Kylie, my sweet child,
I will always and always
Love you.

If the stars should fade away
If the oceans should dry up
And time cease to exist
You can always be
Assured of one thing:
My love for you
Will never fail.
My love for you
Will only ever
Flourish.

A Burning Tree

I think about calling you
My brother.
Think   think   think
About all kinds of crazy
Shit   the type of shit
You'd understand.

Savage, man, beer in my hand
I think about you.
Fighting, pushing, killing
Off all the madness
The rage inside me.

I want to share some words
With you   let you know
I want to.
Damn, brother,
How we stand so far apart.
Apart like the sun
& the moon.

I saw a tree on fire
The other night
And the leaves were falling
To the earth without a thought
In the world.
Dust
Ashes

And the song of time in flames
Meant very little to me.
I picked up my phone
But before I finished dialing
Your number
I hung up.

Now, I tell you, brother
I wanted to talk to you
When I thought
The world
Had
Begun to burn
Down.

As A Nothing

She said to me
"Why do you write so much?
Only a few people read
Your work."

A few or a hundred or a thousand
What does it matter?
She said one day I'll be famous
That the world will remember
The alcoholic poet
That the world will cherish
My work.

I quickly, after our conversation,
Ran to the Arabs, purchased
A can of salvation
And a pack of liberation
And
Got buzzed. The beer
Was cold and the cigarette
Fresh.

Coming from the perspective
Of a hungry poet...
I won't ever let it end
The pen & paper are mine
To be had. And if it is
That not a single person

Reads my work
I'll simply leave the world
The way I entered it
As nothing.

But at least I'll die
Knowing & loving the fact
That I didn't waste my life.
I followed my dream
No matter
The situation
The drugs
The drink
The smoke
& procrastination

I followed my dream.

Mother Murderer

She wanted
Some
Kind
Of sympathy
After
She murdered
Her children.

She had
Put
All of
Them
In her car
That
Morning
And going
Over
100 mph
slammed
her car into
a wall
killing her
children instantly.

She survived!

I have enough
Sympathy

To write
This poem.

Ask me
For anything
Else
Concerning
Her
And I'll say
"Let her die."

Then someone
Will say
But you know
How
It is with
Stress
& depression.

And I'll say
The same way
She put the kids
In the car
To kill them
She could have
Gone to a doctor
And gotten
Help.

The Silence

It's the silence in my work space
That keeps me sane when all
I want to do is abandon this
Obligation to serve a pack
Of wild children that haven't
A clue as to how saying
"Thank you."
Could make my entire day.

It's the silence
That kept me here in this kitchen
For over 8 long-ass torturous years.

The silence and it's not so terrible
So dreadful   so common   so routine.
The food gets cooked & my job
Is accomplished
The children adore me
And it's not so terrible.

The silence
Brings on some form of clarity
Tragic as it may seem having
To work an 8 hour day that never
Changes, never alters,
Something like a factory line
And the children are the parts
I fix

& assemble with
Hot dogs
French fries
Hamburgers
Pizza
Apples
Milk
They take their food and grow.

It's the silence
This unspoken existence
Here in my work place
That allows me to continue
Suffering the madness
Of the children.

My Last Fling

The beer is cold
The cigarette smooth
The anti-depressant affective

I move across my dreams
To this place where I find
You.

There is tomorrow
And another road
Another task
Another shit to flush away.

But whatever may be
Of now and then
Let us face it
Together
Drunk in the knowledge
That we fought
For it
Whatever the hell it may be
Together.
Side by side.

About
The Author /Poet

Joseph Granda-Padron lives in New York City
With his wife and daughter.

He has written one novel entitled *Abstraction* in 2005. He has also published three previous works of poetry: *Veneer* (2005), *Omega* (2007) & *Forgotten* (2007).

www.ingramcontent.com/pod-product-compliance
Lightning Source LLC
Chambersburg PA
CBHW032031150426
43194CB00006B/230